your guide to the law in Scotland

YCPS3

YOUNG CITIZEN'S PASSPORT SCOTLAND

third edition

in association with
the Law Society
of Scotland

young citizen's passport
scotland

your guide to the **law** in scotland

Young people are citizens of today, not citizens in waiting. They should be supported to take up their place in society as responsible, successful, effective and confident citizens, both now and in the future. Central to this is the need to gain an understanding of their rights and responsibilities so they can thrive in the globalised society of the 21st Century.

This book explains those parts of the law that have most relevance to the everyday life of young people in Scotland.

Curriculum for Excellence provides the ideal framework to give children and young people the opportunity to exercise their rights and responsibilities within an educational setting.

I am delighted to be able to support this publication and I would encourage teachers to help make

teaching and learning of the law and a young person's rights and responsibilities more active, relevant and engaging.

Michael Russell
Cabinet Secretary for Education and Lifelong Learning

remember!

In trying to summarise the law, we have had to leave out some details that may be relevant to your own situation. So don't rely on this book as proof of your legal rights. Always take further advice before taking any legal action. Often the best place to start is the Citizens Advice Bureau, but there are many others. Remember too that the law is always developing and changing. To the best of our knowledge we have described the law as it stood in November 2013.

The law is often a blunt instrument and using it in the wrong way can make matters worse. Try to sort things out personally, if you can. It's generally better to use the legal system only as a last resort, when everything else has failed.

HODDER GIBSON
AN HACHETTE UK COMPANY

YCPScotland

The **YCP Scotland** has been produced by the **Citizenship Foundation**, an independent educational charity, which aims to empower individuals to engage in the wider community through education about the law, democracy and society. There are significant differences in certain sections of the law between Scotland and the rest of the UK, and we are grateful to the **Law Society of Scotland** for assistance in producing this Scottish edition of the Young Citizen's Passport.

**The Citizenship Foundation,
50 Featherstone Street,
London EC1Y 8RT**

**Tel 020 7566 4141
Fax 020 7566 4131**

www.citizenshipfoundation.org.uk

**Email
info@citizenshipfoundation.org.uk**

Charity Reg. No. 801360

**The Law Society of Scotland,
26 Drumsheugh Gardens,
Edinburgh EH3 7YR**

**Tel 0131 226 7411
Fax 0131 225 2934**

www.lawscot.org.uk

Email lawscot@lawscot.org.uk

contents

website information and guidance on scots law is available at www.lawscot.org.uk

INDIVIDUALS
ENGAGING IN
SOCIETY

Citizenship Foundation

The Citizenship Foundation would like to thank Hodder Gibson for their support in the production of this Scottish edition.

 Multiple copies of this book have been sent free of charge to all secondary schools in Scotland, thanks to the generosity of the **Law Society of Scotland** as part of their outreach programme. Further copies are available to schools at discounted prices by contacting the Publishers at **hoddergibson@hodder.co.uk**.

Editor and main author Tony Thorpe.

Concept devised by Andrew Phillips OBE, President of the Citizenship Foundation.

We would like to thank Lorna Jack, Liz Campbell and Heather McKendrick at the Law Society of Scotland; Mike Russell, for the foreword; Kay Blaikie, Alan Eccles, John Fotheringham, Stuart Kelly, Claire Kettlewell, Stephen McGowan, Alastair McKendrick, Helen Nelson, William John Rennie, Deborah Elaine Russell, Ayla Skene and Sarah Sutherland.

Designed and illustrated by Nomad Graphique; Mike Gibas, Lena Whitaker, Laura Emms, Mark Askam and Caspar Williams.

Photographs AbleStock, Fotolia, PhotoDisc, PhotoAlto, Nomad Graphique, Ingram Publishing, Lenny Warren/Strathclyde Police, Scottish Executive and John Mitchell. Image of The Mace (page 123), and the Scottish Parliament building (page 124) © Scottish Parliamentary Corporate Body

British Library Cataloguing in Publication Data
A catalogue record for this title is available from the British Library

ISBN 9781444192179

Published by Hodder Gibson, 2a Christie Street, Paisley PA1 1NB.
Tel: 0141 848 1609; Fax: 0141 889 6315; Email: hoddergibson@hodder.co.uk

First published 2004
Second Edition 2007
Third Edition 2013

Impression number	10 9 8 7 6 5 4 3 2 1
Year	2016 2015 2014 2013

Copyright © 2013 by the Citizenship Foundation

Printed in Italy for Hodder Gibson, 2a Christie Street, Paisley, PA1 1NB, Scotland, UK.

young citizen's passport

life

INDIVIDUALS ENGAGING IN SOCIETY

CitizenshipFoundation

Advice and treatment

Consent

A person aged 16 or over can give their own consent to medical treatment. You may also consent to your own treatment if you are under 16, as long as long as the doctor or health professional believes that you understand the nature and consequences of the treatment or advice that you are being given.

Confidentiality

Patients also have a right of confidentiality. Nothing they say to their doctor should be passed on to anyone else - not even the fact that they made an appointment. However, in special cases, information might be shared if the safety of the patient (or someone else) is judged to be at risk.

General practitioners

Everyone living in the UK, including visitors from overseas, is entitled to register with a GP. If you are under 16, this will need to be done by your parent or guardian. A list of local doctors is available from your local Health Board or NHS24, a main post office, library, tourist information office, Citizens Advice Bureau, and also online, see **contacts**.

You have the right to change your GP at any time. You don't have to explain your reasons for doing so or tell the doctor concerned. However, a doctor does not have to accept you as a patient either. If you are refused in this way, the local Health Board has a duty to give you details of local GPs. New patients are entitled to a health examination when they join a practice.

If you are staying for up to three months in another part of the United Kingdom, you can ask to be registered with another GP on a temporary basis. But if you are leaving home and going to college or university, it's probably better to register with a new doctor in the town or city where you are staying, so you are guaranteed all the services of the practice if you ever need them.

It's helpful to provide your medical card or National Health number when you register. If you don't have these, you will need to know your place of birth and the name and address of the doctor or practice with which you were previously registered.

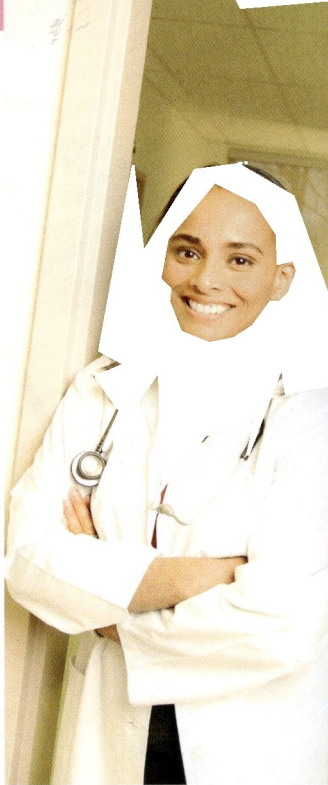

PRESCRIPTIONS

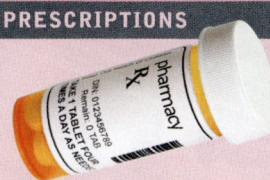

The Scottish Government abolished prescription charges on 1 April 2011.

The abolition of Scottish prescription charges applies only to prescriptions issued on Scottish prescription forms (GP10) and dispensed in Scottish pharmacies. If you have a prescription issued on an English prescription form, you should consult your pharmacist or a Scottish GP for advice on costs for obtaining that prescription in Scotland.

Records Under the *Data Protection Act 1998*, you have a general right to see all your medical records – whether held on paper or computer. You are also entitled to ask for a copy to take away. Access, however, may be refused if the doctor believes that seeing your records may cause you or someone else serious physical or mental harm.

Your GP or the hospital may ask you to pay for this service. The maximum charge to see your records (either on paper or on screen) is £10.00 – and £50.00 if the records are held manually.

If you believe that the information on your records is not correct, you may ask for it to be changed. The doctor does not have to agree, but is required to note on your records what you have said.

OPTICIANS

Free eye examinations are available to all UK residents in Scotland.

In addition, help is also available towards the cost of prescription glasses and contact lenses to anyone who:

- **is under 16,**
- **is under 19 and in full-time education,**
- **needs complex lenses,**
- **is entitled to a valid NHS tax credit exemption certificate,**
- **is named on a valid HC2 certificate issued under the NHS Low Income Scheme,**
- **receives Income Support, income-based Jobseeker's Allowance or income-related Employment and Support Allowance, or the guarantee credit part of Pension Credit or Universal Credit.**

Further information is available online, or from opticians, libraries, and the Citizens Advice Bureau.

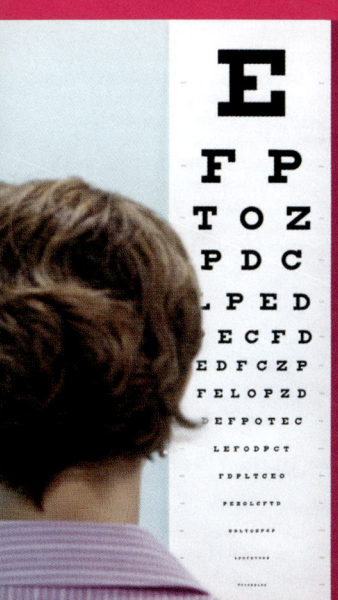

DENTISTS

All British citizens are entitled to dental treatment provided by the National Health Service. However - unlike medical treatment from a GP - dental treatment is not always available free of charge.

Dental treatment is free if:

- you are under 18, or under 19 and still in full-time education,
- you are pregnant or are a nursing mother, or
- you or your partner receive Income Support, income-based Jobseeker's Allowance, or have an NHS Tax Credit Exemption Certificate.

NHS patients pay no charge, for an examination, but there is a cost for treatment such as fillings or extractions, up to a maximum of £384.00 for more complex work.

Dentists can charge a patient who fails to keep an appointment or cancels at very short notice. The level of charge varies from one dentist to another.

Not all dentists provide NHS treatment. To find a list of NHS dentists in your area, look on the NHS website, www.nhs.uk, call NHS Direct (see contacts) or look in the yellow pages, under dental surgeons. You don't have to be registered with a dentist to get NHS treatment; you can contact any surgery providing NHS treatment and ask if they have any NHS appointments available. However, it is usually much easier to obtain treatment if you have regular appointments with the same dentist.

Before each course of treatment, you should receive a treatment plan, showing the work the dentist intends to carry out and what it will cost. The dentist may offer to treat you privately, but should not place pressure on you by implying that the treatment is not available on the NHS. You do not have to accept the treatment being offered.

If you need emergency treatment and are not registered with a dentist, contact a local NHS dentist to see if they can take you on an emergency basis or get in touch with your Local Health Board. Many areas have dental access centres, providing NHS treatment and advice for emergency work and for those not registered for regular treatment. Details are available from your Local Health Board.

NHS 24

NHS 24 is a 24-hour confidential advice and health information service providing guidance on how to look out of yourself and on what to do if you are feeling ill, tel 08454 24 24 24. You may ask for an interpreter to provide advice in your own language.

The NHS 24 Online website provides information about health services, and a variety of medical conditions and treatments, www.nhs24.com.

NHS walk-in centres provide treatment for minor injuries and illnesses seven days a week. You don't need an appointment and will be seen by an experienced NHS nurse. There are centres in many towns and cities. For details of the nearest centre call NHS 24 or visit the National Health Service website, www.nhs.uk, and click on "local NHS services".

use the law with care **try talking first**

Mental health

Most people who receive hospital treatment for a mental illness are there either because they choose to be, and know that they need care, or because they have taken the advice of a doctor or social worker.

In some cases, however, a person who refuses to be examined or treated will be admitted to hospital compulsorily under the *Mental Health (Care and Treatment) (Scotland) Act 2003*. This will be done either in the interests of their own safety or for the protection of others. This process is often referred to as sectioning.

Safeguards This law, also known as the *New Mental Health Act*, contains a number of principles governing the ways in which care and treatment should be provided. The principles are not legal rights, but do indicate how people providing treatment should carry out their duties.

These principles include the need to:

- **take a patient's past and present wishes into account;**
- **make sure a patient gets the information and support they need to take part in decisions;**
- **take into account the views of a patient's carer or guardian;**
- **consider the full range of options for their care;**
- **provide treatment that offers the maximum benefit;**
- **take account of a patient's background, beliefs and abilities;**
- **keep any restrictions on freedom to a minimum in the circumstances;**
- **not treat a patient less favourably than others;**
- **take into account the needs of the patient's carer, and provide them with the information and support that they need; and**
- **take special care of patients who are under 18 years of age.**

Emergency In an emergency, a person can be admitted to hospital for up to 72 hours for their condition to be assessed. This may be done only on the recommendation of a doctor and no treatment may be given, unless in an emergency.

Emergency powers are also available to the police, who can remove someone from a public place who appears to be mentally ill and in need of care. The police officer should take the person to a place of safety, such as a hospital or care home, where they may be kept for up to 24 hours whilst arrangements are made for them to be examined by a doctor.

Leaving hospital Patients admitted for treatment on a voluntary basis can leave hospital whenever they wish, unless this is against medical advice. In these circumstances, nurses have a holding power which allows a patient to be held in hospital for up to two hours so that they can be examined by a doctor.

The procedure for releasing patients who are being detained or treated compulsorily is more complex. Further information is available from the Mental Welfare Commission for Scotland, see **contacts**.

health

Complaints If you have a complaint about the NHS or your treatment, it's important to make it as soon as possible. Advice is available from NHS 24, tel 0845424 24 24, see below.

Tattoos It's illegal for a person to be given a tattoo if they are under 18.

The right to die The law states that a doctor may give a patient a painkilling drug, which shortens their life, as long as the intention is to relieve pain and suffering and not to kill. If the drug is given with the intention of ending that person's life, the doctor can face a charge of murder.

It is possible to make what is called a living will (known in law as an advance directive) setting out how you would like to be treated if you ever lose the capacity to make or convey a decision. You must clearly understand what you are doing when you give the directive and, although it is not legally binding on the doctor, it is an indication of your wishes and will be taken into consideration. An advance directive cannot authorise a doctor to do anything unlawful.

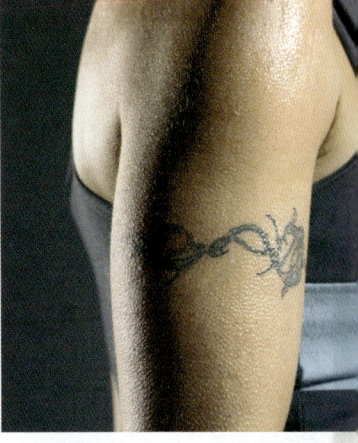

Making a will Anyone aged 16 or over can make a will, provided they are capable of understanding what they are doing. There is no lower age limit for people in the forces on active service, or sailors at sea.

Blood There's no legal minimum age to become a blood donor, but the National Blood Service allows people to give blood if they are in good health, aged 17 or over, and weigh at least 50kgs or 7st 12lbs.

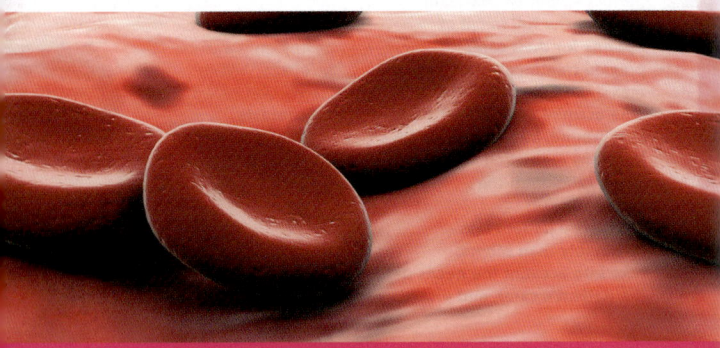

use the law with care try talking first

Controlled drugs

All drugs produce some kind of change in the way a person's body or mind works, and the availability of most drugs – whether aspirins, alcohol or amphetamines – is controlled by law.

The main law covering the use of dangerous drugs in the UK is the *Misuse of Drugs Act 1971*. This Act controls the use of such drugs and it is an offence to possess, produce or supply anyone with them. Controlled drugs are divided into three categories in law – classes A, B and C. Class A are considered to be the most dangerous.

CLASS A DRUGS

Cocaine is a white powder that is injected, rubbed onto gums, or snorted through a tube. Crack is cocaine treated with chemicals, to allow it to be smoked. Both give a high, followed by a rapid down. The only way to maintain the high is to keep taking the drug – but regular use leads to sickness, sleeplessness, weight loss, and addiction.

Heroin is made from the opium poppy and can be smoked, sniffed or injected. It comes as a white powder when pure. Street heroin is usually brownish white. Heroin slows down the brain and, at first, gives a feeling of total relaxation. Repeated use creates dependency. Overdosing causes unconsciousness and often death – particularly if used with other drugs, such as alcohol.

LSD, also known as acid, is a man-made substance, sold impregnated on blotting paper (often printed with cartoon characters or in colourful patterns) and dissolved on the tongue. It usually takes about an hour to work, and lasts up to 12 hours. The effects depend on the strength of the dose and the user's mood. It generally distorts feelings, vision and hearing, and bad trips lead to depression and panic, or worse, if the user is already anxious.

Ecstasy, or E, is usually sold as tablets of different shapes and colour. It makes the user feel friendly and full of energy, and sound and colours can seem much more intense. However, the comedown can leave the user tired and low – often for days. Regular users can have problems sleeping, and some women find it makes their periods heavier. Ecstasy affects the body's temperature control and it may cause the user to overheat and dehydrate. There is no guarantee that tablets sold as ecstasy do not contain some other ingredients. This can make their use unpredictable and dangerous.

drugs and the law

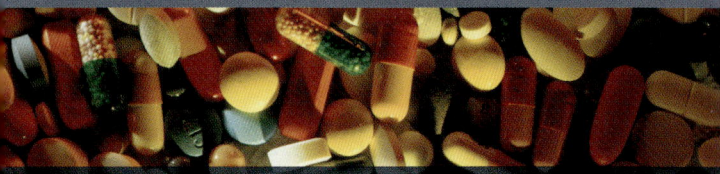

Amphetamines, sold as pills or powder, were developed to treat depression. They give a feeling of energy and confidence, but increasing doses are needed to keep up the effect. The downside is anxiety, insomnia, irritability and less resistance to disease and, as with all illegal drugs, there is no guarantee that they do not contain other harmful substances.

Barbiturates are used in medicine to help people who cannot sleep. They produce feelings of drowsiness and relief from anxiety. They are sold as a powder or coloured capsule. Regular use creates dependency. They are extremely dangerous when taken with alcohol or other drugs.

Cannabis, now reclassified as a Class B drug, carries a maximum penalty of five years' imprisonment and an unlimited fine for possession. A sentence of up to 14 years and an unlimited fine may be given for dealing in and supplying cannabis.

People over 18 found possessing cannabis are likely to receive a warning and have the drug confiscated, but could be arrested if smoking in public. Repeat offenders face arrest and prosecution.

Someone under 18 caught with cannabis is likely to be arrested, taken to a police station, and given a final warning, reprimand, or charge, depending on the seriousness of the offence and whether they have been in trouble before for a similar offence. If they receive a warning they will be referred to the local youth offending team.

The effects of cannabis vary from one person to another. Some feel relaxed and happy, but the downside can be moodiness, anxiety, and difficulties with memory. Heavy users risk severe tiredness, mental health problems, and cancer from the drug's chemical constituents.

Mephedrone and naphyrone (also known as NRG-1) have caused recent concern, leading to their classification as Class B drugs. Both substances are now banned and carry a penalty for possession of up to five years in prison or an unlimited fine, and up to 14 years in prison for supplying the drug.

CLASS C DRUGS

Tranquillisers cause lower alertness, and affect people who drive or operate machinery. A number of **anabolic steroids** are also on the list of controlled drugs after concern over their misuse in sport and bodybuilding.

use the law with care try talking first

The risks

• There is no way of knowing exactly what is in drugs made or obtained illegally. This makes them unpredictable and dangerous.

- All drugs have side effects that may be dangerous and even fatal – particularly if they are mixed or taken regularly.

- Anyone using shared needles, filters or spoons, risks becoming infected with hepatitis or HIV, the virus that leads to AIDS.

- Hepatitis C is a newly discovered virus that can cause severe long-term liver damage. It is caused by blood-to-blood contact, generally through sharing needles when injecting drugs.

- Illegal drug-taking places a person's job, school, or college place at risk. Employers and head teachers have a legal duty to confiscate drugs found at work or school, and hand them to the police as quickly as possible.

- Although drug use is not a criminal offence in the UK, it is an offence to possess or supply controlled drugs.

Possession

Possession of any quantity of a controlled drug is a criminal offence, even if it's only a tiny amount. First-time offenders in possession of Class C drugs are likely to receive a reprimand or warning.

Supply

It is an offence under the *Misuse of Drugs Act 1971* to supply or to offer to supply someone with a controlled drug. Obviously this includes the sale of drugs – but it is still an offence even if money does not change hands. Giving a controlled drug to a friend, or sharing a drug at a party by passing it from one person to another, is still seen in law as supply. (See **leisure**, page 92.)

It is also an offence if the substance sold is not actually a controlled drug, but the seller claimed or believed it to be one.

Production

It is an offence under the *Misuse of Drugs Act 1971* to produce any controlled drug. This includes letting someone use your kitchen or a room for this purpose.

Growing cannabis comes under this heading, and is a criminal offence if it can be established that the accused knew what they were doing.

drugs and the law

Police powers

If a police officer has reasonable grounds to suspect that someone is in possession of a controlled drug, the officer can search that person and their vehicle and seize anything that seems to be evidence of an offence.

Glue sniffing

The effect of solvent abuse is rather like getting drunk on alcohol. However, it takes effect more quickly as the substances enter the bloodstream through the lungs rather than through the stomach. People sniffing glue may experience hallucinations and, if plastic bags are used, risk falling unconscious or choking on their own vomit. Glue sniffing itself is not against the law, but it is an offence to supply a solvent to anyone if there is reasonable cause to believe that the fumes might be inhaled.

It is also an offence to sell lighter fuel to anyone under 18.

Tobacco and alcohol

It is an offence both to sell tobacco products to someone under 18, and also for an under 18-year-old to try to buy cigarettes, tobacco, cigarette papers etc. Anyone over 18 who tries to buy tobacco products for someone under 18 also commits an offence.

Since 2006, smoking in public places that are entirely or substantially enclosed has been forbidden; this also includes the majority of workplaces.

It is illegal to sell alcohol to anyone below the age of 18. For more details on this, see **leisure**, page 87.

Information

Know the Score is a free Scottish helpline providing information and advice on drugs, 24 hours a day, http://knowthescore.info, or tel 0800 587 587 9.

use the law with care **try talking first**

<table>
<tr><td>

Not the whole story

</td><td>

Although sex is discussed much more now than it was in the past, most people at some stage in their

</td></tr>
</table>

lives get confused about what they should and should not be doing. Probably the best advice is:

- **don't believe everything you hear,**
- **decide what is right for you and your partner,**
- **talk to your partner and think about their point of view.**

You don't have to do anything that you are not comfortable with. Nor should you expect your partner to. There is no golden age by which you should have had sex. Some people will choose not to because they are not interested, or because there hasn't yet been the right opportunity, or because they want to wait until they are married. There's plenty of time and it's OK to opt out.

Pressurising someone into going further than they want, as well as being morally wrong, can reach a stage where it is also against the law. For example, even kissing or touching someone without their agreement can be an assault. In law, both people must agree to what they are doing (known as consent), and they must understand what is happening. The person who gets someone drunk in order to go to bed with them, or takes advantage of their

drunken state, risks being charged with rape, see **safety**, page 23.

<table>
<tr><td>

Age of consent

</td><td>

Unlawful sex

Under the *Sexual Offences Amendment Act 2000*, the age of consent for boys and

</td></tr>
</table>

girls is 16; this age applies to lesbian, gay, and heterosexual relationships. However, the age of consent becomes 18 years of age in cases involving sexual activity between a young person and someone in a position of trust, such as a teacher or care worker. Even if the young person agrees to the relationship, the age of consent nevertheless remains at 18.

Any kind of sexual activity between someone who is over 16 and someone under 16 is unlawful. If the sexual activity has not involved oral or penetrative sex, and the young person is 13 or over, it may be a defence for the adult to say that they believed the other person to be aged 16 or over.

It is illegal for young people who are both under 16 to have oral sex or sexual intercourse, even if they both consent.

Grooming Under the *Protection of Children and Prevention of Sexual Offences (Scotland) Act 2005*, it is an offence for an adult to meet or to travel to meet a child, who is (or the adult believes to be) 16 years of age, or younger, with the intent of carrying out unlawful sexual activity.

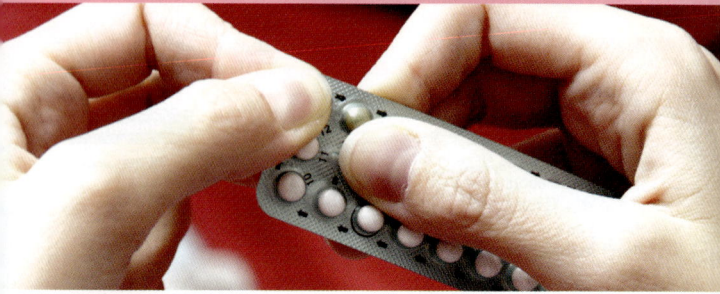

Lesbian and gay relationships

Since 2001, the age of consent has been the same for gay men and women as it has for heterosexuals. The law no longer criminalises any relationship where both people consent, and are aged 16 and over.

There are still difficulties for lesbian and gay people in a society where some people and faiths do not fully recognise a person's right to a gay relationship.

If you need to talk to someone who understands, see **contacts** for groups who may be able to help.

Contraception

Each person who has sex is responsible for guarding against the risks to both people. It is important to know how to use contraceptives properly and how they affect your body. Good advice is therefore vital.

For this you can go to a family planning clinic, your doctor, or to a Brook Advisory Centre. Your school may also have a school nurse who you could talk to.

If you're under 16, a doctor can prescribe contraceptives for you without telling your parents - as long as the doctor believes that you are mature enough to understand what is being proposed.

Condoms can easily be bought from supermarkets, garages, and chemists, from slot machines in toilets, and by mail order. Femidoms, which are a form of sheath for women, are sold in chemists. Both these and condoms are available free from family planning clinics.

Emergency

If you have had sex without using contraception – or used a condom that split – emergency contraception is available to stop you from becoming pregnant.

This form of contraception is for emergencies only. It is not as reliable as the pill or condom, and does not protect against sexual diseases. Some people also believe that it represents a form of early abortion.

The emergency contraceptive pill is available free from your GP or a family planning clinic, and should be taken within 72 hours of unprotected sex. It can also be bought from most chemists – but some do not sell it to girls under 16.

The British Pregnancy Advisory Service now prescribes the morning after pill in advance of need, see **contacts**.

use the law with care try talking first

You think you're pregnant

Your period is late and you think you might be pregnant. What do you do? To find out if you are expecting a baby, you can:

- **see your doctor;**
- **speak to someone you trust – your partner, a family member or friend;**
- **buy a pregnancy testing kit from a chemist (these are generally accurate and cost between £4-£15);**
- **visit a family planning clinic or Brook Advisory Centre, who will offer confidential advice and a free test with an immediate result.**

What if it's positive?

You will have three choices: to go through with the pregnancy and bring up your child; to give the baby over to be adopted; or to have an abortion and terminate the pregnancy.

This can be a hugely difficult decision. It is vital that you do everything possible to make the right decision, for much hangs upon it. So talk, if you can, to your partner in the pregnancy, your parents, good friends, and your doctor.

Adoption

Giving up a baby for adoption is not easy - for the mother or father. It's best to talk to someone about this, such as your doctor or someone at the antenatal clinic, as soon as possible.

The adoption will probably be handled by a social worker who will discuss the kind of family the birth parents want their child to grow up in and will try to find out as much as possible about the birth family to pass on to the adopters. Under the *Adoption and Children (Scotland) Act 2007*, married, unmarried, and couples in a civil partnership, can apply to adopt a child. A key factor is the ability to provide a stable and loving home for the child.

Neither birth parent has the right to see their child after she or he has been adopted, although sometimes the court can give permission for contact. Once they reach 18, a child may seek to get in touch with their birth parents, and birth parents may trace their child through an intermediary service. Help and advice for anyone affected by adoption is available through the British Agencies for Adoption and Fostering, see **contacts**.

Abortion

A decision by a woman to have an abortion involves practical considerations about how having a child is likely to affect her future, her current relationships, and her responsibilities. It is also likely to involve questions of feelings and values. Some people have strong objections to abortion, based on their personal beliefs, family, culture or religion, believing that an unborn baby has a right to life in all (or almost all) circumstances.

For anyone thinking of having an abortion it is almost always helpful to talk to someone about it. This can be a doctor, staff at a family planning clinic, or someone from one of the organisations listed in **contacts**.

The law

Abortion in Scotland is controlled by the *Abortion Act 1967*. This states that an abortion may be legally carried out if two doctors agree that:

- **continuing the pregnancy would risk the life of the mother; or**
- **the mother is less than 24 weeks pregnant and that the risks of physical or mental injury to her or her existing children would be greater by continuing with the pregnancy; or**
- **there is a substantial risk that the child will be born severely handicapped.**

Concern over the mother's mental health is a common reason for doctors to allow an abortion – particularly if they feel she is likely to suffer excessive emotional strain.

Ninety per cent of abortions in Britain take place within the first 13 weeks of pregnancy, although abortion is legal up to 24 weeks and after that, only in the exceptional circumstances listed above.

If an abortion takes place, the procedure that the doctor will follow will be largely determined by the stage of the woman's pregnancy. A medical abortion, involving two clinic visits and two doses of medication, is normally performed within the first nine weeks. An aspiration abortion, in which the contents of the uterus are drawn out, is undertaken using a local anaesthetic. In these circumstances doctors insist that a capable person accompanies the patient to and from the hospital or clinic.

Consent

A young woman under 16 may be referred for an abortion without her parent's consent if doctors agree that she is mature enough to understand the procedure involved. However, the doctor will advise and help the young woman to talk to her parents or carer, who should be able to provide valuable support once they have overcome any initial shock or concern.

The earlier an abortion takes place, the safer it is. It is also easier to arrange and more likely that it can be provided locally. Most areas can provide abortions up to twelve weeks; after this, it may be necessary to travel to a large town or city.

The father, whether he is married to the mother or not, has no right to prevent the mother from having an abortion.

A doctor does not have to carry out an abortion if it is against his or her conscience. If this happens, you can arrange to see another doctor.

What is HIV?

To understand HIV (human immunodeficiency virus), you have to know something about the immune system that stops us from becoming ill.

Blood plays an important part in our body's defence against illness. It contains millions of cells, about one per cent of which are white cells. A particularly important type of white cell is called the T-helper cell, and one of the jobs of these cells is to fight off infection.

HIV is a virus that attacks the T-helper cells. If it grows inside these cells, and other germs get into our body, we have no way of fighting infection. We become ill and develop what is called acquired immune deficiency syndrome, known as AIDS.

HIV is the cause of AIDS; although not everyone who is HIV positive goes on to suffer the effects associated with the syndrome.

How do you get HIV?

The HIV virus is found in the blood, semen, or vaginal fluid of a person with HIV or AIDS. Infection takes place when these fluids pass from an infected person into the bloodstream of someone else. This can happen in several ways:

- **by having unprotected sex with someone who already has the HIV virus. This means putting a penis into a vagina or anus without using a condom. The risk of contracting HIV infection through unprotected oral sex is thought to be much lower - but transmission is possible if semen, vaginal fluid, or menstrual blood come into contact with bleeding gums or mouth infections. You can help to protect yourself from HIV infection through sex by using a condom or dental dam.**
- **by sharing or using a hypodermic needle that has already been used by someone with HIV, leading to the exchange of a small amount of infected blood;**
- **as a result of a mother with HIV passing it on to her baby whilst it is growing inside her.**

Blood transfusions in industrialised countries should be safe as the blood used is routinely screened.

Anyone who feels they may be at risk of HIV or AIDS should seek medical advice and help, see **contacts**.

How don't you get HIV?

The HIV virus dies quickly once outside the body. Because of this, you don't get HIV from:

• hugging • kissing, including French kisses • sharing towels or cutlery • swimming • toilet seats • sharing musical instruments • giving blood.

HIV and the law

It is a serious offence for someone who knows they are HIV positive to have unprotected sex with a partner, without telling them that they are infected. If the partner contracts HIV as a result, the carrier may be charged with causing grievous bodily harm and, if found guilty, face a term of imprisonment.

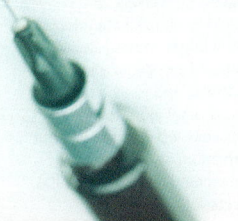

hiv and aids

There are a number of sexually transmitted infections (such as chlamydia, gonorrhoea, hepatitis and syphilis) that are caught from sexual contact with people who have the infection themselves. Some infections cause sores and pains in or around the area of your sexual organ, but others can affect different parts of the body. Hepatitis, for example, causes an inflammation of the liver and may be transmitted by unprotected penetrative or oral sex.

If you have any concerns, see a doctor straightaway, and don't have sex with anyone until the condition has cleared up, otherwise you put your partner's health at risk as well as your own. Seeking urgent treatment for STIs could save you from suffering from permanent health problems in the future.

However, not all STIs show signs of infection. Anyone who has sex with someone who is not their regular partner is particularly at risk, especially if they fail to use a condom. Chlamydia, for example, can pass undetected for some time, but may eventually produce pain and discomfort, and cause infertility in men and give women problems in conceiving.

Advice and treatment on sexually transmitted infections is available from clinics dealing with family planning, pregnancy or genito-urinary medicine, as well as family doctors. The appointment is entirely confidential, although if you are under 16, the doctor may be reluctant to do anything without consulting your parents. If this is the case, it is worth checking first.

HIV and work

It has been against the law since 2005 for an employer to discriminate against an employee with HIV/AIDS. It is also now unlawful, under the *Equality Act 2010*, for employers to ask applicants health-related questions at their interview or to ask them to complete a health-related questionnaire. Employers may, however, ask people applying for work about their access requirements and whether they can do all the things that are central or essential to the job.

A person with HIV or AIDS is under no legal obligation to tell their employer about their condition, but the government advises healthcare workers who believe themselves to be at risk from infection to seek medical advice immediately. An employer must keep information of this kind confidential, and is, as a rule, not entitled to tell other workers that an employee is infected with HIV without his or her permission.

If you are worried about HIV or AIDS, see **contacts** for help.

Prostitution

Prostitution itself (that is selling sex) is not illegal, as long as takes place between two consenting adults. However, it is an offence under the *Civic Government (Scotland) Act 1982* for a sex worker (male or female) to loiter or try to solicit business in a public place.

It is also an offence under the *Prostitution (Public Places) (Scotland) Act 2007* to loiter in a public place in order to obtain the services of a prostitute or to solicit these service from a vehicle or from public transport.

It is also illegal to pay anyone under the age of 18 for sexual services. If the police become aware that a young person under the age of 16 is involved in prostitution, they will almost certainly inform Social Services who will decide whether to apply for an order to take that person into care.

safety

INDIVIDUALS
ENGAGING IN
SOCIETY

CitizenshipFoundation

violent crime

Arrest – doing it yourself

If you see someone committing a serious offence or have reasonable grounds for believing that they have committed one, you can make a citizen's arrest. But, take care. People have been hurt and even killed trying to do their civic duty.

If you do get involved, remember that an ordinary person only has the power to make an arrest for a serious offence - such as theft, serious assault, or burglary. Don't arrest someone for parking on a double yellow line. You can't arrest someone who you think is about to commit an offence (it must already have been done), nor can you use excessive force.

The best advice is to take in as much as you can about the incident, and then to ring the police.

Fighting back

If you're threatened or hit, it's usually better to try to avoid a fight by talking to your attacker or backing off calmly.

If you can't do this, the law says that you can use reasonable force to defend yourself. This means that you're entitled to fight back, but not to go over the top and beat up the other person. If you do, you will have also committed an offence.

There is no law that says that you must report a crime to the police. However, if you want to claim compensation for your injuries, the crime must first have been reported to the police.

Self defence

If you carry something to use for self-defence, you run the risk of actually breaking the law yourself. Under the *Criminal Law (Consolidation) (Scotland) Act 1995*, it is an offence to carry something made, or adapted, to cause injury to someone. This includes things like a knife, bicycle chain, or a sharpened comb. The penalty is a prison sentence, or a fine, or both.

Knives

Under the *Criminal Law (Consolidation) (Scotland) Act 1995*, it is an offence to have anything with a blade or sharp point in a public place. Folded pocket knives are allowed as long as the blade is less than 3" long. It is, however, a defence if the knife is for use at work, part of a national costume, or being carried for religious reasons.

Schools are specifically mentioned as places where articles with blades or points must not be carried, and the police have the power to enter and search school premises if they have good reason to believe that an offence of this kind has been committed. The penalty is a prison sentence or fine.

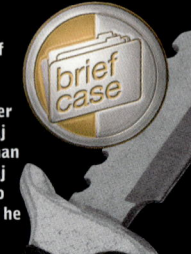

BRIEF CASE: Raj

Raj ran an off-licence, and had twice been the victim of armed robbery. One night, a man carrying a long knife came into the shop demanding money from the till. As Raj was being held with a knife to his throat, his brother came through from the back and the robber ran off. Raj was so angry that he got into his van and chased the man down the street knocking him down and killing him. Raj was found guilty of manslaughter and sentenced to two and a half years' imprisonment. The Court decided that he could not have been acting in self-defence because he was, by that time, not being attacked or threatened.

use the law with care **try talking first**

Victims of violent crime

Victims of violent crime can apply to the *Criminal Injuries Compensation Authority* for compensation for their injuries. Violent crime is not strictly defined, but it usually means a physical attack or a period of abuse. Close relatives and dependants of victims who have died can also apply for compensation.

The crime must be reported to the police as soon as possible, and an application for compensation made within two years of the incident that caused the injury. However, an exception may be made if, for example, the delay in reporting was caused by the after effects of the crime. The crime must be serious enough to receive at least the minimum award of £1,000, but compensation may be reduced if, for example, the victim had a criminal record or their behaviour contributed to the injury.

Victim Support gives advice to victims of crime. Their helpline number is available online and in the local phone book, see **contacts**.

If you are a victim of crime and called as a witness, you can arrange to see a courtroom before the case starts, have a seat reserved for someone accompanying you, and ask to wait separately from other people. Details are available from the *Scottish Court Service* and *Victim Support Scotland*, see **contacts**.

SOME WORDS THEY USE

Assault & battery
Assault in law is an attack on one person by another, with the intention of causing bodily harm (even if very little force is used). It also takes place when a person causes someone to fear that they are about to suffer immediate unlawful physical violence - for example, by the use of threatening gestures or words.

In Scotland there is no distinction as in England and Wales between various types of assault, though there is an offence of aggravated assault where a weapon is used.

Theft by housebreaking and opening a lockfast place
Theft by housebreaking, takes place when a person enters any building by forcing their way in by, for example, breaking a window or forcing a door. Theft by housebreaking does not occur, however if the thief gains entry by opening an unlocked door or climbing through an open window. The crime does not apply to forcing open a car, a safe or a locked room within a house. This is known as opening a lockfast place.

Even if nothing is taken or done, a crime has still been committed. It's enough in law to prove that the person intended to break the law in this way.

Robbery
Stealing something with the use or threat of force.

Breach of the peace
This is refers to conduct likely to cause alarm and disturbance.

harassment

Abusive behaviour It is an offence to use threatening, abusive, or insulting words or behaviour in public in a way that is intended to cause a person harassment, alarm, or distress. It's also an offence to put up a sign or a poster that is threatening or abusive in the same way. This kind of conduct in Scotland is likely to amount to the offence of breach of the peace.

Under the *Criminal Justice and Licensing (Scotland) Act 2010* it is also an offence for someone to behave in a threatening or abusive manner in a way that would be likely to cause a reasonable person to feel fear or alarm

Under the *Criminal Law (Consolidation) (Scotland) Act 1995*, there is also a separate offence of racially aggravated harassment. It is also an offence to harass someone on the basis of their religion.

The law is designed to protect anyone who is being treated like this because, for example, of their race, disability, religion, or sexuality. Harassment of this kind is a crime and can be reported to the police, who have a duty to investigate and to try to find those responsible. Statements from witnesses will strengthen a case.

Punishment for offences that can be shown to be racially or religiously aggravated, such as harassment, assault and criminal damage, carry increased penalties.

Local councils also have a number of powers they can use to help tenants or homeowners in their area who are being racially harassed or attacked. They can prosecute residents for harassing or causing nuisance to other residents, they can get a court order, such as an ASBO, stopping people committing certain types of anti-social behaviour, or, if those responsible are council tenants, they can evict them from their home.

■ BRIEF CASE: Marcia

brief case

Marcia and her 10-year-old son were not the only black people on their estate, but for some reason faced almost continuous trouble from one particular group of boys. Marcia first tried ignoring the problem and then spoke to the boys and tried to talk to their parents. Nothing worked. Eventually she complained to the council who investigated the case and obtained a court order requiring the parents of one of the boys to leave their house, which they rented from the council. The boy's parents appealed, saying it was not their offensive behaviour but that of their son. The appeal was dismissed. The judge said that Marcia and her son should not be deprived of their rights just because the parents could not control their son.

Stalking Under the *Criminal Justice and Licensing (Scotland) Act 2010*, the offence of stalking occurs when someone, on a number of occasions, behaves in a way that causes another person to feel fear or alarm, or provokes a breach of the peace.

Someone who feels they might be a victim of harassment can apply to a court, for what is known as an interdict, ordering the person committing the offence to keep a certain distance from the victim's house or place of work.

use the law with care **try talking first**

What if it happens to me? It all depends on the situation. If it's an isolated incident, and the person is someone you don't know, then it may be best to try and ignore it. If you react and get abusive yourself, you run the risk of finding yourself in a far worse situation.

However, if it's happened before, or you're being harassed where you live, then it's important to tell the police - for your own safety.

If you are getting abuse at school, college or at work, try and sort it out with the people concerned, but if that's not possible, or successful, raise it with someone in authority, who will have a legal duty to help you. See also **equal rights**, pages 44-46.

Someone suffering serious abuse or harassment may be able to claim compensation from the *Criminal Injuries Compensation Authority*, see page 148.

Abusive telephone calls and messages It is an offence under the *Communications Act 2003* to make malicious and threatening phone calls, or to send messages that are very offensive, indecent or menacing.

If you get such a call, try not to react, just hang up. If the phone rings again, don't say anything – a genuine caller will speak first. If you get such texts or messages, don't delete them; instead, report the matter to the police and your service provider or site administrator.

sexual assault

Sexual assault It is an offence to touch or threaten a person in an indecent way. Groping and unwanted fondling can come into this category. Indecent assault can carry a punishment of up to life imprisonment.

It is also an offence to spike someone's drink and to watch or photograph someone without their consent when they are involved in a private act.

Rape If a male, aged eight or over, has intercourse with another person, and either that person doesn't want him to or the male does not care if they are consenting, then he has committed the crime of rape. Intercourse can include forced penetration of another person's vagina, mouth or anus. It is also an offence to threaten or force someone to have sex against their will, or to give them drugs in the hope that they will give in.

Previously under Scottish law, rape could only be committed by a man on a woman;

however, the *Sexual Offences (Scotland) Act 2009* gave legal recognition to male rape.

Going out with someone is not, in law, an invitation to have sexual intercourse with them. Forcing another person to have sex is rape, and it is no defence for the perpetrator to say that they were drunk. It is also rape if the victim had too much alcohol or other drugs to know what they were doing. A wife does not have to have sex with her husband; if she does not consent, it is rape.

sexual assault

If you are raped Although you may not want to tell anyone, police stations should have officers who have been trained to deal with victims of sexual offences in a sensitive way.

If you are a woman, you can ask to be examined by a female doctor and you can take along your parents or a friend.

The police will be able to gather evidence more easily if you report the rape or assault as soon as possible.

Once a victim tells the police that they have been raped or sexually assaulted, or the suspect has been charged, the victim has the right in law to remain anonymous. The victim cannot be questioned in court by the accused, nor can their name and address or picture be reported in the media. Attempted rape is dealt with in the same way.

Help is available from *Victim Support Scotland*, local *Rape Crisis Centres*, and *Survivors UK*, who will talk to any person who has suffered an unpleasant sexual experience, see **contacts** for further details.

Accused of rape If you are accused of raping someone, rightly or wrongly, you should immediately contact a solicitor. Rape is a serious crime, and the punishment can be severe.

keeping safe

There are some simple steps that both men and women can take to make themselves safer.

- **If you go out - especially at night - tell someone where you are going.**
- **If possible, stay away from known danger spots.**
- **Keep your drink within your sights at all times.**
- **If you're out late, get a lift back if you can with someone you trust, or book a taxi, see page 91.**
- **If you walk home, try to get someone you know to walk with you.**
- **Try not to have expensive possessions like mobile phones on show.**
- **Check on the security of your home. Ordinary bolts and chains are not expensive.**
- **Knowing some self-defence can give you a feeling of greater confidence.**

- **If you carry a screech alarm keep it ready in your hand, not in your pocket or handbag.**
- **Men can help by taking care not to frighten women. For example, if you're walking in the same direction as a woman at night, don't walk behind her, cross over the road and walk on the other side.**
- **If you are facing some kind of harassment, tell someone about it. Ignoring it can make you more vulnerable.**

CONTACTS see pages 146–153 for organisations able to give help & advice young citizen's passport

education

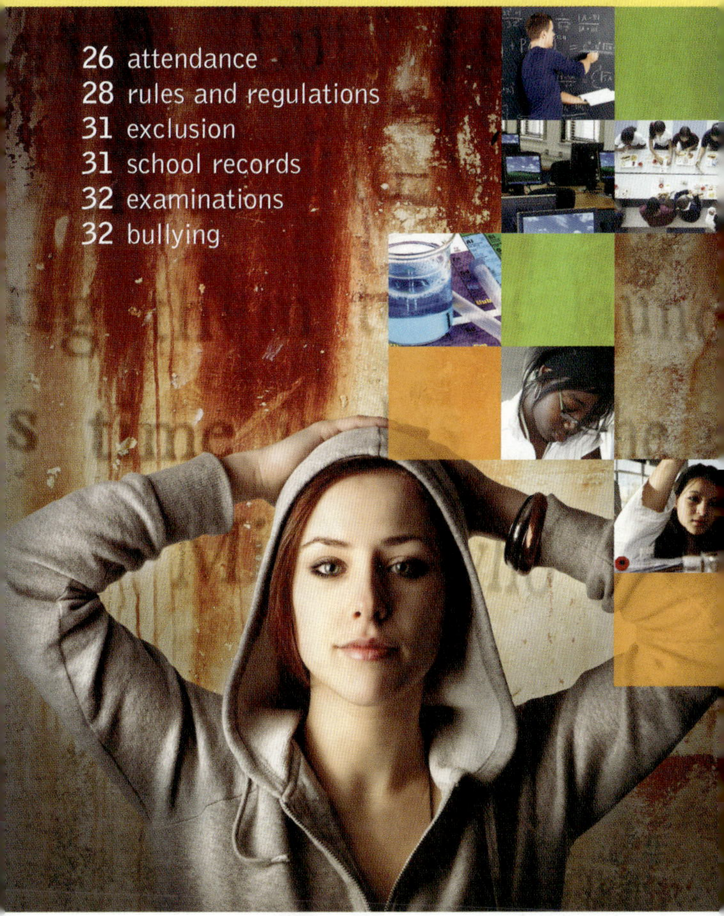

INDIVIDUALS ENGAGING IN SOCIETY

Citizenship Foundation

Under the *Education (Scotland) Act 1980*, it is the duty of the parent of every school age child to provide what the law describes as "an efficient education "… suitable to his age, ability and aptitude, either by causing him to attend a public school regularly or by other means".

The words "by means" are important because the law allows parents to educate their children either at school, as most people do, or at home.

If a child is already in school, and their parents wish to educate them at home, they must first get permission from the local authority before withdrawing them from school. Permission should only be refused if there is good reason for concern.

Which school?

Each school has a given catchment area, and education authorities normally offer school places to all children living in that area. Parents (but not children) have the right to request a place at a school outwith the catchment area, and education authorities have a duty to meet this request, if there are places available. However, a child may be refused admission if the school is full or if the school (for example, a special school) is not seen to be appropriate for the child's needs.

In most areas, education authorities also offer the choice of denominational (religious) schools which are open to all.

If admission to a particular school is refused, a Letter of Refusal is issued. Parents (but not children) have a right to appeal against the decision. Details of this process should be given in the Letter.

Further information is available in the Scottish Government's guide for parents, *Choosing a School* or from the Parentzone website, see **contacts**.

Parents who cannot agree between themselves on a choice of school can ask a court to decide where their child will be educated. In these circumstances, the court must also listen to and respect the wishes of the child concerned.

Starting school

Children generally begin primary school at the age of five. Depending on their birthday, they may begin school at a slightly younger or older age, as all children begin on the same date (in August). A child is assumed to be of school age on the first school start date following their fifth birthday. However, some parents of children who would ordinarily begin school before their fifth birthday may delay their child's school start date until the following August.

Help with the costs

State education is free and it is unlawful for schools to try to make parents pay for books or equipment that pupils need for subjects or activities taken in school hours as part of the school curriculum.

However, some charges may be made for:

- **materials for practical subjects,**
- **optional trips taken outside school hours,**
- **some school trips, even if the activity is part of the school timetable.**

The local education authority has a duty to provide pupils with free school transport or passes if their school is not within walking distance (for children aged eight and over, this is three miles from their home) or where the route home is unsuitable, or it involves crossing a dangerous road.

However, these are not available if the child has been offered a place in a suitable school that is closer, but which their parents have turned down.

Local authorities may also offer grants to assist with school clothing. These are usually awarded dependant on the family's income.

An Education Maintenance Allowance scheme for 16 to 19-year-olds is available to young people from low income families who are attending a full-time course at school or college.

Free school meals

Pupils at school are entitled to free school meals if their parents (or they themselves) receive Income Support or income-based Jobseeker's Allowance, some types of Tax Credits, or support under the *Immigration and Asylum Act 1999*.

Pupils who bring a packed lunch must be provided with somewhere appropriate to eat it.

Leaving school or staying on

Compulsory education ends at the age of sixteen. By law, young people whose sixteenth birthday falls between 1st March and 30th September may leave school on 31st May of that year. Young people whose birthday falls between 1st October and the last day of February the following year may leave school at the beginning of their school's Christmas holidays.

Once you have reached compulsory school age, your parents cannot force you to stay on at school against your wishes. You are also entitled to remain at school until your eighteenth birthday.

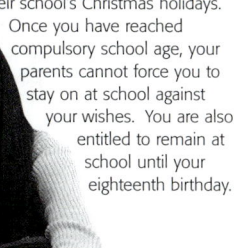

attendance

Truancy

Parents have a legal duty to make sure that their children attend school regularly or are suitably educated elsewhere. If they fail to do this, they may be committing a criminal offence and may be prosecuted. Every education authority has a Children's Panel made up of people from across the community, and a child who does not attend school regularly may be referred to them. The panel can decide on measures to be taken to help the child get back to school, such as imposing supervision or sometimes removing the child from the home, depending on the reasons for the hearing.

rules and regulations

Religious worship and education

The law states that all pupils in Scotland (including those between 16 and 18) should receive religious education and religious observance. Parents may withdraw their children from these classes, but this must not interfere with the attendance of the pupil at school. Pupils cannot opt out of religious education or worship themselves - it must be done by their parents.

Sex education

The law states that all secondary schools must provide sex education for their pupils and in a way that recognises the moral issues involved. Scottish Government guidance states that the purpose of sex education is to provide knowledge and understanding of the nature of sexuality within the context of relationships based on love and respect.

Learning about relationships, sexual health, and parenthood begins early on in primary school right up to S4-S6. Schools should equip children and young people with information on a wide range of issues, depending on their age and stage. These could include puberty, sexually transmitted infections (STIs), contraception, and accessing sexual health services.

Government guidelines encourage teachers to involve parents and other appropriate professionals if they are asked for help by a pupil with a sexual or relationship problem

If parents or carers feel that the lesson content is not appropriate, they can withdraw a child from all or part of a planned programme, and alternative arrangements should be made for the pupil.

use the law with care try talking first

Punishment

All schools should have a student behaviour policy, which should be regularly reviewed and outlined to pupils, parents and staff. Teachers have the legal power to discipline pupils for breaking school rules, but punishments must be reasonable.

Detention

Schools may keep pupils in detention during school hours. If a teacher wishes to keep a child in after school, he or she should first obtain the parent's agreement.

The decision to keep a pupil in detention must be reasonable in the circumstances and pupils should not be held in detention for too long; nor should their safety be put at risk if, as a consequence, they miss the last bus home.

Confiscation

Teachers may confiscate any forbidden items, such as mobile phones, jewellery etc, which they should keep safe and return to the pupil after a reasonable time.

If illegal drugs or weapons are found, teachers must confiscate the items and hand them over to the police.

School uniform

A report by the then Scottish Executive, called *Better Behaviour - Better Learning*, recommended that every school should agree a dress code with parents and pupils. Once this has been agreed it becomes a school rule, and disciplinary sanctions can be imposed if pupils do not wear the uniform.

Grants may be available to assist families with the purchase of school uniforms.

CORPORAL PUNISHMENT

Corporal punishment is banned in all schools in Scotland – although there are circumstances under law when a member of staff may be required to use reasonable force to prevent a pupil from injuring themselves or someone else or damaging property.

However, a teacher who uses excessive force may have committed an assault, which could lead to the police charging them with a criminal offence.

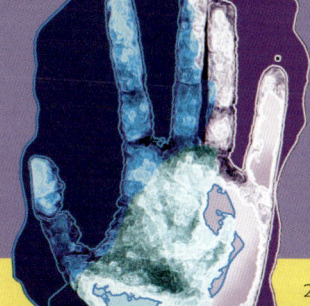

rules and regulations

DRUGS IN SCHOOL

Schools are required to make clear to pupils and parents what action will be taken if a pupil is found to be involved in any way with unauthorised drugs within the boundaries of the school. The term 'unauthorised drugs' includes tobacco and alcohol, as well as illegal drugs, and the 'boundaries of the school' may include journeys in school time, work experience, and school trips.

Pupils can be excluded from school temporarily or permanently if caught with illegal drugs, but this should not be automatic, even though using or possessing drugs are criminal offences. Schools should deal with cases individually and take into account the circumstances surrounding each incident.

Although it will be important in most cases to tell parents of their child's involvement with drugs, schools are not legally required to do so.

Schools do not have to act on rumours that a pupil is taking drugs in or out of school, but head teachers should inform the police when illegal drugs are found on a pupil or on school premises. A teacher cannot always guarantee confidentiality for a pupil who might privately explain that he or she is taking drugs.

The law allows a teacher to search a student's locker or desk, if he or she suspects that it contains illegal drugs or any other unlawful items. A pupil who is believed to be in possession of illegal drugs can be asked to empty their pockets. If they refuse, the police can be called to deal with the situation. A teacher should never carry out an intimate search.

If a head teacher decides to call the police, efforts must be made to contact the pupil's parents. A young person under 16 should not be interviewed by the police without a parent, adult friend, or social worker being present.

A young person is also entitled to legal representation during an interview, and this must be offered to them.

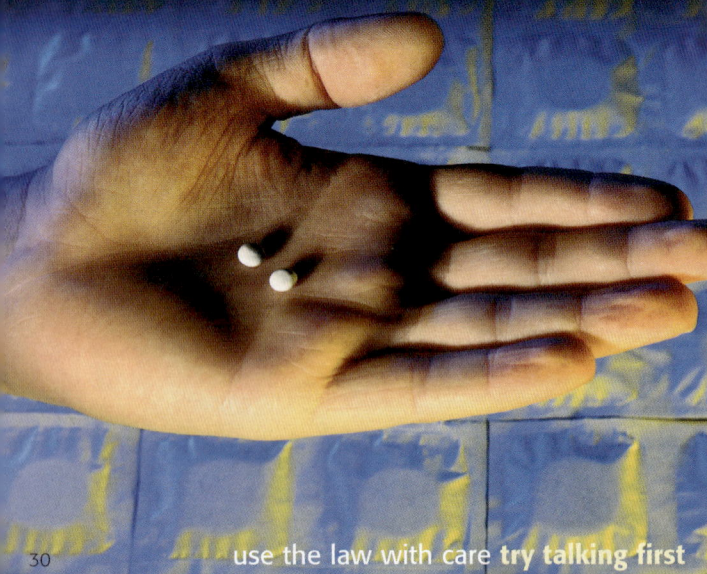

use the law with care **try talking first**

EDUCATION
exclusion

A pupil may be excluded from school if either:

a) **their parent(s) are breaking school rules or disciplinary requirements or encouraging or allowing the pupil to do so; or**

b) **allowing the pupil to remain at school would be seriously detrimental to order and discipline at the school or the educational wellbeing of the pupils there.**

Guidance from the Scottish Government says that exclusion should only be used as a last resort. A pupil who breaks the law should not automatically be excluded without considering the individual circumstances of the case. A temporary exclusion is usually for a set length of time lasting from a half-day to several weeks.

When pupils are excluded from school, their parents must be told without delay, and should receive a letter explaining the reasons for the decision, how long the exclusion it will last, and how they can appeal against it.

Parents, young people and children with legal capacity (usually, age 12 or over) have a right of appeal against the exclusion. The appeal is heard by an education appeal committee. There is a further right of appeal to the Sheriff Court.

When a pupil is excluded from school, the school (or education authority) should provide them with alternative education instead (eg sending work home, home tuition, or allocating them to a new school).

Further details may be obtained from the Parentzone website, see **contacts**.

school records

Under the *Data Protection Act 1998*, pupils of any age have the right to see their school records. They need to put their request in writing, and the request should only be turned down if the pupil does not understand what he or she is asking for.

Under the *Pupils' Educational Records (Scotland) Regulations 2003*, parents also have had the right to see their child's educational record. They do not need to pay to read the record, but may be charged a small fee if they want to keep a copy.

However the school may withhold certain items if it feels they might damage the mental or physical health of the pupil or someone else. Some sensitive personal information might not be disclosed to parents on the grounds of pupil confidentiality.

When making a request to see your school records, you can ask for the information to be supplied in an alternative language or form. This should be supplied, as long as the education authority feels that your request is reasonable.

examinations

The vast majority of Scottish pupils sit exams administered by the Scottish Qualifications Authority. If a pupil is refused permission to sit a public exam, their parents may appeal to the school against this decision.

Anyone caught cheating in a public exam is likely to be disqualified and the examination board may decide not to mark any of the candidate's papers. Candidates disqualified for cheating have a right of appeal to the exam board. It is an offence to impersonate someone in an exam. Both the impersonator and the person being impersonated can be charged.

If a candidate does not do as well as expected in an exam, the school may ask for their paper to be checked at the appeal stage to make sure that the marks have been correctly assessed. Certain costs may be involved in this which parents might have to fund.

There is very little that can be done for a candidate who does badly in an exam because of poor teaching or a failure by a teacher to follow the correct procedure – or even the right syllabus. The examining board gives grades based on the candidate's actual performance. If an education authority has been negligent in their education of a pupil, compensation may be available. However, action through the courts for compensation can be costly and has no guarantee of success.

bullying

Schools have a legal duty to make sure students are safe in school, including on their journey to and from school. All schools must have an anti-bullying policy and policies protecting students from racial or sexual discrimination, and must act immediately on any evidence of a pupil being bullied. If they do not, they may be sued for negligence. It is possible for a pupil to take legal action against another pupil to put a stop to bullying.

Schools are entitled to exclude pupils permanently who are persistent bullies and, in serious cases, may inform the police. See **contacts** for further details.

Safety

The education authority has a duty to take reasonable care of pupils while they are under their charge. On a school trip this can apply for 24 hours a day. The standard of supervision required depends on the nature of the activity and the age or capability of the pupils.

If the action of a teacher is called into question, the test applied by the court is to ask, "did they act in a way in which no reasonable teacher would have acted?"

Schools also have responsibilities for their pupils under health and safety legislation. This is part of the criminal law and is enforced by the Health & Safety Executive.

INDIVIDUALS
ENGAGING IN
SOCIETY

CitizenshipFoundation

part-time work

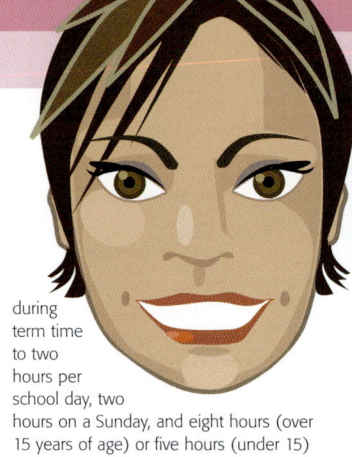

At what age?

The law controlling the work of young people below school leaving age varies from one local authority to another.

Under the *Children and Young Persons (Scotland) Act 1937*, each local authority creates its own by-laws setting out the kinds of work that young people may do. Most by-laws require employers to inform the council about, and hold permits for, all young people they employ.

Generally, it is only children aged 13 or over who are permitted to work; and the only kinds of employment they can be given is light work, such as work in a hairdresser, office, shop (ie shelf stacking), or delivering newspapers. The categories of work permitted vary from one local authority to another.

Restrictions are also imposed on the hours a young person can work. Under the *Children (Protection at Work) (Scotland) Regulations 2006*, any child below minimum school leaving age may work no more than twelve hours per week during term time.

The regulations also limit working hours during term time to two hours per school day, two hours on a Sunday, and eight hours (over 15 years of age) or five hours (under 15) for any other day, eg Saturday.

There are few restrictions on the employment of 16 or 17-year-olds. However, people under 18 cannot normally work in a bar, unless they work in a restaurant where drinks are served with meals, or they are being trained for the licensing trade under a Modern Apprenticeship scheme.

Copies of the by-laws controlling the employment of young people in your area can be obtained online and from the local library and council office.

■ BRIEF CASE

HEALTH & SAFETY

A boy of 15, working in a butcher's, suffered severe injuries when his arm was trapped in a mincing machine from which the guard had been removed. The court fined the owner and manager of the shop more than £20,000.

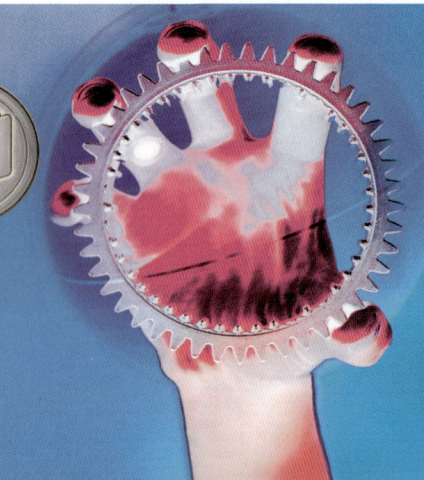

| Employment rights | **Today, many of the rights of those in part-time jobs (even if it's only for a few hours per week)** |

are now the same as those in full-time employment.

If you are in part-time work you:
- are protected by the anti-discrimination laws, regardless of how many hours you work or how long you have worked for your employer;
- have the right, if you have worked for your employer for one month, to be given notice if asked to leave and, after two months to receive the terms and conditions of your job, in writing;
- are entitled to redundancy pay if you are made redundant and have worked for your employer for at least two years from the age of 18; and
- are entitled to claim for unfair dismissal if you have worked for your employer for at least a year, and feel you have been unfairly sacked.

The *Part-time Workers (Prevention of Less Favourable Treatment) Regulations 2000* state that part-timers must receive the same treatment as full-time workers in relation to their hourly rates of pay, training, holiday, and maternity rights, etc..

training

| Youth training | Skillseekers offer work-based |

training to young people leaving full-time education. The programme is designed for 16 and 17-year-old school leavers, but is also open to those who have left full-time education and would be able to complete their training by the age of 25. All Skillseekers work towards a nationally recognised Scottish Vocational Qualification (SVQ).

Training can last up to three years, but this is flexible, and depends on individual ability, and the type of qualification and training that you do.

Alternatively, Modern Apprenticeships offer those aged over 16 paid employment combined with the opportunity to train for jobs at craft, technician, and management level.

training

Pay

You may be taken on as an employee or a work-based Skillseekers trainee, undertaking the programme because you are unemployed and looking for work. As an employee, you will receive at least the minimum wage (see page 41). Apprentices do not qualify for the minimum wage until they are 19 or have completed a year of their apprenticeship, whichever comes later. If you are a trainee, you will receive a training allowance and help with the cost of travel and accommodation, if training away from your home.

Terms and conditions

Whether you are an employee or a work-based trainee, you are entitled to receive written details of the terms and conditions of your training. If you are employed you are covered by all the

other rights and benefits mentioned in this chapter.

If you are a work-based trainee you will also be given an individual training plan that will explain:

- **how your training will be organised;**
- **the date when your programme begins and ends;**
- **what time will be spent in the workplace and college or training centre;**
- **details of the SVQ for which you are training.**

If you are not happy with your training, you may be able to transfer to a different programme with the same trainer or to another one. If your trainer cannot finish your training, you should be given the opportunity to transfer to another trainer with a similar training programme.

If you are absent for more than the period specified in your terms and conditions, without permission from your trainer, your training programme will end.

Skills Development Scotland or your local enterprise company should be able to give you details of apprenticeships in your area.

Equal opportunities

Trainees have the same protection as other workers against unfair discrimination. Help is available at your careers office and the local Citizens Advice Bureau. For more information, see **equal rights**, page 44.

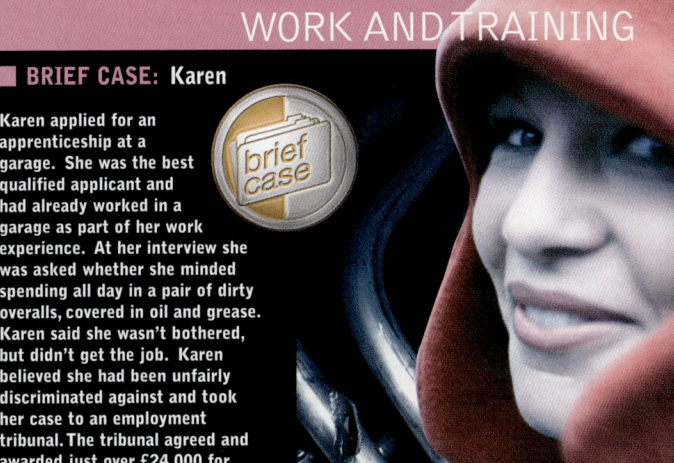

BRIEF CASE: Karen

Karen applied for an apprenticeship at a garage. She was the best qualified applicant and had already worked in a garage as part of her work experience. At her interview she was asked whether she minded spending all day in a pair of dirty overalls, covered in oil and grease. Karen said she wasn't bothered, but didn't get the job. Karen believed she had been unfairly discriminated against and took her case to an employment tribunal. The tribunal agreed and awarded just over £24,000 for loss of earnings and injury to her feelings.

Health and safety

Your trainer or employer must make sure that the place where you work is safe, and you have a legal responsibility to follow all safety procedures and use equipment in the way instructed.

If you have an accident, or are worried about safety, speak to your supervisor immediately. If you are injured or become ill while training, you should also contact your local Benefits Agency office.

Anyone injured while training may be able to claim Industrial Injuries Disablement Benefit. Contact your local Benefits Agency office for details.

Problems

When you start training you should be told what to do if you have any problems while on the programme. If you are unhappy with the training you can discuss it with your supervisor or see the careers officer, who may be able to help solve the problem or find you more suitable training.

Non-employed trainees are not entitled to any notice if they are dismissed, nor can they take their case to an employment tribunal if they feel they have been sacked unfairly. But if they are offered another job, they don't need to work out their notice before leaving. Employed trainees or apprentices receive the same legal protection as other employees and should give whatever period of notice is stated in their contract of employment.

ycp scotland

Applications

Read through the application form before starting to fill it in. Draft your longer answers, until you are happy with what you have written.

All the information you give should be correct. An employer is usually entitled to dismiss someone who is deliberately misleading on their application form or at interview.

Referees

You will need the names of two people who are prepared to act as your referees, to write a short report or reference about you for an employer. One referee is usually your last employer, or the head teacher or year tutor in your school. References must be factually accurate and should not create a misleading or unfair impression of the person concerned.

Your CV

Some adverts for jobs tell you to send for an application form, others will ask for a letter with your curriculum vitae, usually known as a C.V. This is something that you write or type, giving personal details, qualifications, experience, and interests. Make several copies and don't forget to keep one yourself.

Application form

Please fill in ALL the boxes below in BLOCK CA
If you miss something out it might delay your
Remember to read the Agreement conditio

Step 1 – Your personal details

Title   Surnam

First name

Are you?   Male   Female

Nationality

Interviews

If you've not been to the office or building before, leave yourself extra time to find it; or go round and find out where it is beforehand. If you can't make the appointment, phone or write to explain, and ask for a more convenient time.

Have a few questions ready to ask - about what the course or job involves. If they offer you a place or job, before you accept try to think if there's anything else you need to know. If there is, ask.

Everyone at work has a contract - whether full or part-time, permanent or fixed term.

A contract is another word for the agreement between you and your employer, spelling out the arrangements that will affect your work - such as pay, hours, the sort of job you will do, holidays, and the notice you have to give, or you can expect to receive, when your employment comes to an end.

Terms and conditions

If you are to be employed for more than a month, your employer must give you a written statement within two months of you starting work, setting out the terms and conditions of your job.

This statement should give...

- **your name and that of your employer;**
- **your job title and place of work;**
- **your starting date;**
- **your rate of pay, and details of how and when you will be paid;**
- **your hours of work;**
- **your holidays and holiday pay;**
- **arrangements for sickness, sick pay and pension;**
- **details of the firm's disciplinary procedures, and how complaints at work are dealt with; and**
- **the amount of notice that you or your employer must give if your contract is to be ended.**

Any changes to your statement should be given in writing.

contracts

Apart from your written statement, the terms of your contract do not have to be written down. They can be agreed verbally – but it's a good idea to have things in writing, in case there's disagreement about what you're expected to do.

Check your contract carefully. Make sure you agree with what it says and that it covers everything you are being asked to do. If it is different from the agreement made at your interview, point this out. Keep safe all pay slips, letters and papers you are given by your employer.

Take care

If you agree to do something on a regular basis that is not written into your contract - like working on a Saturday - you may be, in law, agreeing to a new term or condition of work. If you decide later that working every Saturday is not a good idea, your boss may be entitled to insist that you continue. By turning up for work six days a week, you may have actually changed your contract by your conduct.

Internet and email

Under the *Human Rights Act 1998* and the *Regulation of Investigatory Powers Act 2000*, employers are entitled to set reasonable rules for their workers using email and the internet at work.

Employers may forbid staff from writing or reading personal emails at work or from browsing websites for personal interest, and can monitor what they do. However, employees should be informed that checks of this kind will be made.

An employer who opens an employee's email without a good business reason may be infringing that person's right to privacy (see **human rights**, page 128), and emails may also be open in extreme circumstances to check, for example, whether the law has been broken.

Pay

Your wages will either be agreed between you and your boss or else based on rates agreed between employers and the trade union. Either way, your employer must give you a detailed written pay statement each time you are paid, showing exactly what you are being paid and how much is being taken off in tax, national insurance etc. It is up to your employer to choose how you are paid. This can be by cash, cheque, or straight into your bank account.

Your rate of sick pay must be explained in your contract. It will probably say either that you will be paid at your standard rate for a certain length of time, or that you will be given statutory sick pay. This is set each year by the Department for Work and Pensions and is usually lower than your normal pay. If you are off sick for four or more days in a row (including Sundays and bank holidays) you will receive statutory sick pay from your employer for up to 28 weeks. You don't have to claim statutory sick pay, just follow your employer's rules for notifying sickness.

You can check what you should receive in leaflets available from Benefits Agency offices and libraries.

MINIMUM PAY

The *National Minimum Wage Act 1998* sets minimum rates at which people should be paid. The minimum rate payable (2013/14) for people aged 21 years and over is £6.31 per hour, 18-20 years of age £5.03 per hour, and 16-17 years of age £3.72 per hour. The minimum wage for apprentices is £2.68 per hour. The minimum wage is updated every year in October.

If your employer fails to grant you your legal rights you may take your case to an employment tribunal. Further help is available from the Pay and Work Rights Helpline, tel 0800 9172368.

Hours

Your hours of work will normally be agreed between you and your employer, although there are some jobs where these are limited by law for reasons of health and safety.

The *Working Time Regulations* set maximum limits of eight hours a day or 40 hours a week for young workers ie those aged between the minimum school leaving age and 18. These hours cannot be averaged and you can only work longer than this if there are no adult workers available, and if working will not adversely affect your training needs.

For workers over 18, the maximum working week of 48 hours, including overtime, can be averaged over 17 weeks. You can agree to do more than this, but your employer cannot pressurise you to do so.

You are also entitled to:

- **a rest break of 20 minutes when you work for more than six hours at a time (or 30 minutes every four hours if you are under 18); and**
- **at least eleven consecutive hours off in any 24 hour period (twelve hours off, if you are under 18).**

Workers who are under 18 may not ordinarily work between 10pm and 6am. Some night work is allowed in certain jobs, such as the armed forces, farm work, catering, working in a pub, restaurant or hotel, working in a bakery, newspaper delivery, and retail trading. However, an adult must supervise the work, and rest periods must be given. Workers who believe that the hours they are expected to work do not follow the regulations can take their case to an employment tribunal.

HOLIDAYS

The *Working Time Regulations* give most people over 16 the right to at least 28 days' paid holiday a year. During the first year of employment, you have the right to take one twelfth of your annual holiday entitlement for each month worked. Some jobs are not fully covered by the Regulations, for example, the police and armed forces.

health and safety

Safety

Employers have a legal duty to take care of the safety of their staff. If they don't, they are breaking the *Health and Safety at Work Act 1974*.

This means that the equipment that you use must not be dangerous or defective, and that the people you work with must work safely and responsibly.

Your duty is to follow safety regulations and to take care of your own and other people's safety.

If you work for a firm where there are five or more employees, your boss must give you details of the health and safety arrangements in writing.

If you are worried about health and safety, raise the matter with your supervisor. Your employer may not dismiss you or treat you unfairly for raising genuine concerns, as long as you follow the right procedures. If you remain concerned, contact the local offices of the Health and Safety Executive. Your local Citizens Advice Bureau will be able to tell you how to do this.

■ BRIEF CASE: Maria

Maria worked as a waitress in a holiday centre. Her staff chalet was in poor condition, with mould growing on the walls, no heating, and a very dirty mattress.

One morning, Maria felt unwell and noticed a rash on her right arm. She went to the doctor who said it had been caused by an insect bite, possibly fleas.

Maria complained to her boss who arranged for the chalet to be decontaminated. Maria moved back a few days later, but was bitten again, and once more complained.

Shortly afterwards Maria was told that the centre was over-staffed and she was dismissed. Maria believed that the real reason for losing her job was her complaint about health and safety. An employment tribunal agreed, and awarded Maria compensation for unfair dismissal.

brief case

use the law with care **try talking first**

■ BRIEF CASE: Tragic accident

A worker at a food warehouse at Inchinnan, Renfrewshire, was injured when a container he was loading with waste food toppled over and broke his ankle. He was treated and then released from hospital but died three weeks from complications from his injuries. His employer was fined £67,000 for failing to provide a safe and risk-free system of work.

brief case

Accidents

If you are injured at work, report the matter to your supervisor straightaway and, unless the injury is very small, see a doctor. Make a note of what happened, check to see whether you are entitled to any welfare benefits, and get legal advice from either your trade union or a solicitor. You may be entitled to compensation for your injuries.

Using a computer screen

If you have a problem with your eyes that you think might be due to using display screen equipment at work, your employer has a duty to arrange for you to have an eyesight test if you ask for one, and to do whatever they reasonably can at work to reduce further problems. This is all part of a general requirement for employers to check on the health and safety risks to people using computer screens at work, contained in the *Health and Safety (Display Screen Equipment) Regulations 1992.*

equal rights

Discrimination

Over the last 40 years, the law has gradually provided more and more protection against discrimination at work. Discrimination law applies to all aspects of work, including applications for a new job, terms and conditions of work, conduct in the workplace, and references given when someone is still at work, or has left.

In 2010, most of the different laws (for example the *Race Relations Act 1976*, the *Equal Pay Act 1970*, the *Sex Discrimination Act 1975*, the *Disability Discrimination Act 1995*, the *Employment Equality (Sexual Orientation) Regulations 2003* and the *Employment Equality (Religion or Belief) Regulations 2003*) were brought together under the *Equality Act 2010*, protecting people from discrimination on grounds of age, disability, race, religion or belief, sex, and sexual orientation.

Age

It is against the law to discriminate against someone at work because of their age. Generally speaking, a person should not be turned down for a job because they are too old or too young, and employers should not advertise jobs for particular age groups or in a way that may discourage candidates in particular age groups from applying.

Disability

For more than ten years, it has been against the law for any employer to treat a person less favourably on grounds of their disability, unless the treatment can be justified. Employers are also required to make reasonable adjustments to the working environment or to a person's role in order to enable a person with disabilities to be employed.

Race

It is against the law to discriminate against someone because of their colour, race, nationality, or ethnic origin.

■ BRIEF CASE: Eugene

Eugene suffered constant racist taunts from other workers on the building site where he worked, and the management did little to stop it. They said that "black bastard" and "nigger" were words often used on sites. The tribunal decided that Eugene had been directly discriminated against and awarded Eugene damages for the treatment he had received.

■ BRIEF CASE: Susan

Susan, a train driver on London Underground, was forced to hand in her notice when new shift rosters meant that it was impossible for her to work and look after her three-year-old child. She took her case to an employment tribunal, complaining of sex discrimination. The tribunal decided that the new working arrangements indirectly discriminated against women because more women were single parents.

use the law with care **try talking first**

Religion An employer may not treat an employee less favourably than others because of their religion or belief; nor should employers have rules or practises that put someone at a disadvantage because of their religion or belief. For example, employers generally do not have the right to compel a person to dress in a particular way that is against their religion or belief, unless there is a justifiable reason to do so (for example, health and safety).

Sex It is against the law to treat a person less favourably because of their sex. This rule applies to all employers, regardless of the number of people they employ. Woman and men also have the right to equal pay for the same or similar work.

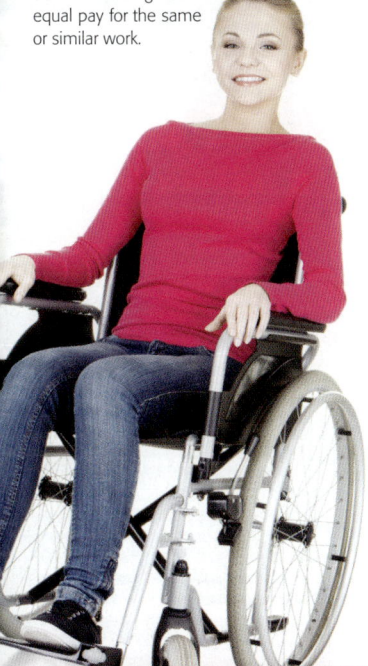

Sexual orientation Since 2003, it has been against the law to discriminate against someone at work because of their sexuality or perceived sexuality. Employers may not treat gay, lesbian, heterosexual or bisexual employers less favourably than any other employee.

Help and advice If you feel you have been a victim of unfair discrimination at work, you can get help from your local Citizens Advice Bureau, Law Centre, trade union or from a solicitor.

Advice and information on most matters of discrimination on the grounds of age, disability, race, religion or belief, sex and sexual orientation is available from the Equality on Human Rights Commission, see **contacts**.

If you can't sort out things informally, you may be advised to take your complaint to an employment tribunal. This must be done within three months. If you are successful, the tribunal can award damages to compensate you for the losses you have suffered. You may be able to settle your case without the need to go to court but, if not, be prepared for a long and difficult battle, and remember to take legal advice.

Harassment at work

The law also allows employees to make a claim against their employer if they face harassment at work because of their age, disability, race, religion or belief, sex, or sexual orientation.

Harassment refers to unwanted behaviour towards someone that they find intimidating, offensive, or demeaning. Examples might include:

- **unwanted advances or physical contact,**
- **insulting remarks, or**
- **comments on a person's looks.**

It is an employer's duty to take steps to prevent these things from happening. If you face difficulties of this kind it's usually better, if you can, to try to sort things out informally. But if the harassment continues, don't be afraid to complain using your employer's grievance procedure. It's not always easy to prove harassment, but judges are prepared to award damages when the victim can show that they have suffered some financial disadvantage and/or injury to their feelings from the harassment.

■ BRIEF CASE: No fun

An employment tribunal decided that a secretary, who was sacked when she complained about being groped by a senior member of staff at a Christmas party, was unfairly dismissed. She was awarded £4,700 in damages.

■ BRIEF CASE: Offensive and degrading

Janine worked with a group of men who regularly looked at pornography on their computers at work. Their boss knew this was going on, but did nothing to stop it – even though Janine had told him that it made her feel very uncomfortable. Eventually Janine made a complaint of sexual harassment to an employment tribunal. The tribunal decided that the men's behaviour was degrading and offensive to women and that their employer should have taken steps to stop it. The company was ordered to pay Janine compensation for the damage she had suffered.

maternity and family rights

Maternity rights

Female employees who are expecting a baby or adopting a child have certain minimum legal rights – although some employers may provide more than these. You can check your position from your contract. Employees in this situation should not be treated less favourably at work for any reason connected with their pregnancy or decision to adopt.

Time off with pay for antenatal care

This applies to full and part-time workers, and it makes no difference how long you have worked for your employer. Your employer cannot insist that you make up the time, or that you take the appointment in your free time.

Maternity leave You are entitled to 52 weeks' maternity leave no matter how long you have worked for your employer, and whether you are full or part-time. You also have the right to return to the same, or similar, job after your maternity leave.

All benefits, except pay, listed in your contract, continue throughout the first 26 weeks of ordinary maternity leave – including medical insurance, pension, and even a company car, if you have

one. You can agree to work up to ten days during your maternity leave to keep in touch with your workplace.

Correct procedures If you don't follow the correct procedures in applying for maternity leave, you risk losing certain maternity benefits, such as the right to maternity pay after your baby is born. For example, you must give notice to your employer by the end of the 15th week before your baby is due. The personnel department at work, your trade union, or local Citizens Advice Bureau can explain what you need to do.

Maternity pay You are entitled to statutory maternity pay for the first 39 weeks of your maternity leave including the time you take off before your baby is born, provided you have worked for your employer for a sufficient length of time and earn, on average at least £107 per week.

Your maternity pay will probably be lower than your usual rate, unless it says otherwise in your contract. If you are on a low income or have not worked for long enough to qualify for maternity pay, you may still be entitled to a maternity allowance from the Benefits Agency.

maternity and family rights

Paternity leave A father has a right to take up to two weeks' paid paternity leave. This must be taken in one block and is only available to employees who have worked for 26 continuous weeks for their employer. Statutory pay is paid at the same rate as the standard statutory maternity rate.

Parental leave Both parents have a right to take up to 13 weeks' unpaid parental leave over the first five years of their child's life, provided they have worked for their employer for at least a year. Parents of disabled children are entitled to 18 weeks' unpaid leave over the first 18 years of their child's life. Changes in the law in 2015 will give working parents much more flexibility in how they share the care of their child during the first year after birth.

Time off Regardless of how long you have worked for your employer, you have the right to take unpaid time off for urgent family problems, such as an accident or sudden illness, but you must give your employer the reasons for your absence as soon as possible. You may only take a reasonable amount of time, and should let your employer know when you expect to return.

Right to request flexible working If you have 26 weeks' service, and are a parent of a child aged 16 or under, or of a disabled child under 18, you have the right to ask your employer for more flexible working hours in order to look after your child. From April 2014, the right to request flexible working hours will be extended to all employees who have been with their employer for 26 weeks or more.

trade unions

Membership It is up to you whether you join a trade union. Trade unions don't only negotiate wages for their members. They also give advice, inform members of their rights, and act on their behalf over difficulties with their employer. An employer must not sack someone for either belonging or not belonging to a trade union.

Not all employers want to work with unions. But, if there are more than 20 people working for an employer, a trade union may be able to force the employer to recognise the union and to negotiate with them.

Industrial action If you take industrial action - for example, by stopping work - you may be breaking your contract. However, if the strike has been lawfully organised and correctly balloted, your employer is not entitled to dismiss you for taking part. This is automatically unfair and you may have a case for compensation. But you cannot claim unfair dismissal if you are sacked for taking part in an unofficial strike.

use the law with care **try talking first**

If you're sacked or made redundant, your legal rights mainly depend on how long you have been working for your employer.

Notice Unless you have done something very serious and committed what's known in law as gross misconduct - such as theft or fighting - your boss should not sack you on the spot. Your contract should state the notice to which you are entitled, and this usually depends on how long you have been working for your employer.

After one month's employment, either side should give one week's notice. After two years' employment, your employer should give you two weeks' notice, three weeks' after three years, and so on, up to twelve weeks' notice for employment which has lasted twelve years or more.

However, your notice period might be longer if this is stated in your contract, and your employer may decide to pay you instead of letting you work out your notice. Before dismissing you, your employer must follow certain procedures, designed to promote discussion about your position.

Reasons in writing If you are fired by your employer, for whom you have worked for more than one year, you can ask for a written statement of the reasons for your dismissal. Your employer must provide this within 14 days.

Redundancy This happens when an employer no longer needs the job done for which you were employed. Your rights mainly depend on your age and how long you have worked for the firm.

If you are made redundant, you have a right to redundancy pay, if you:

- **have worked for your employer for a continuous period of at least two years since you were; and**
- **have not unreasonably turned down an offer of another job from your employer.**

If your employer has gone bust, you may be able to get a redundancy payment from the Redundancy Payments Service, see **contacts**.

If you are made redundant, get advice from your trade union, Citizens Advice Bureau or a solicitor as soon as possible. If you feel that the way you were chosen for redundancy was unfair or unreasonable, you may also be able to claim unfair dismissal.

losing your job

UNFAIR DISMISSAL

If you feel that you have been unfairly dismissed, and have worked for your employer continuously for a year or more, you can make a complaint to an employment tribunal.

Even if you've not been sacked, but leave your job because of the behaviour of your employer, you may have a claim for unfair dismissal. This is known in law as constructive dismissal, but will only be successful if you can show that your employer has broken your employment contract. If you are thinking of resigning because of this, keep a record of what is happening and, before you hand in your notice, write to your employer explaining your reasons for leaving.

Take legal advice before you make a claim for unfair dismissal. Your trade union, local Citizens Advice Bureau or a solicitor can help. If you are unhappy about your dismissal, don't delay in seeking assistance. You only have three months in which to make a complaint.

If the tribunal agrees that your dismissal was unfair, your employer will probably be ordered to pay you a sum in compensation. This is a basic award, which is calculated on the basis of your age, weekly pay and length of service, plus a figure for compensation.

There are no limits to the damages you can receive if you lose your job as a result of unfair discrimination, if you are dismissed unfairly, or if you are selected for redundancy for reasons connected with matters such as health and safety.

■ BRIEF CASE: Sacked

Jeannette's son was ill in the night and Jeanette overslept the next morning. When she arrived late at the café where she worked, she was sacked. She explained what had happened, but her boss took no notice. Jeannette took her case to an employment tribunal, who decided that she had been unfairly dismissed, as she had not been given a warning or a second chance.

■ BRIEF CASE: Redundant

Business was bad and Dean was made redundant from his job at a petrol station. He was given £520 redundancy pay, but soon realised that his job was now being done by the boss's son. Dean hadn't been redundant at all, and so won his claim for unfair dismissal.

money

INDIVIDUALS
ENGAGING IN
SOCIETY

CitizenshipFoundation

It's a contract

When you buy something from a shop or pay for a service (like a train fare or haircut) you are making an agreement, known in law as a *contract*.

The contract means that, in return for the money that you pay, the goods you buy should do everything you can reasonably expect and, in particular, all that the seller and manufacturer claim.

Once a contract has been agreed, neither side can change it on their own. Some shops allow customers to opt out of their contract by agreeing to exchange unwanted items or by providing a refund, as long as goods are returned in mint condition with the receipt. Shops don't have to do this by law, unless it was promised as part of the contract.

But what about your rights if the goods you have bought are faulty?

The Sale of Goods Act

The law applying to most everyday purchases is the *Sale of Goods Act 1979* – an important Act that has been extended over the last 30 years. It says that when you buy goods from a shop or trader, they must …

…be of satisfactory quality

This means that they must be free from faults and not scratched or damaged, and equally applies to goods bought in a sale. However, this rule does not apply if the fault was pointed out by the sales assistant or if you inspected the item and had a good opportunity to discover the fault.

Second-hand goods bought from a shop or trader must also be of satisfactory quality.

…be fit for all their intended purposes

This means that they must do what the seller, packaging or advertisements claim. A watch sold as waterproof should not stop if you forget to take it off in the shower.

Neither of the protections above apply if you bought the goods privately (eg through a 'small ad') – when the buyer is responsible for deciding the quality of what she or he wants to buy.

…match the description

The goods must be the same as the description on the packaging or advertisement, or given by the assistant at the time of sale. A bracelet marked solid silver, must be just that.

This rule also applies to second-hand goods, including those sold privately.

GETTING IT RIGHT

If you're buying something expensive, it's wise to do some research beforehand. Many products can be checked out via online reviews or specialist magazines.

You can also go to a shop and ask just to see an item, without buying it. If you decide to make a purchase, keep the receipt in case you have a complaint.

Services too

Dry cleaners, shoe repairers, hairdressers, travel agents and many others provide a service - and you are protected by law if that service is inadequate.

Under the *Supply of Goods and Services Act 1982*, a service must be provided:

- **with reasonable care and skill;**
- **within a reasonable time; and**
- **for a reasonable charge.**

Problems? Problems are less likely to occur if certain things are agreed before the work is started. How much will it cost? How long will it take? What happens if the work can't be finished? Try to sort these out first.

Handle your complaint just as you would were it for faulty goods. Don't be afraid to seek advice. Help is available from your local Citizens Advice Bureau or consumer advice centre.

Some trades, such as travel agents, garages, dry cleaners, shoe sellers etc. have their own associations laying down a code of practice or standards. These have no legal standing, but the associations can help you resolve your complaint against a trader. Contact addresses are available online and from your local library.

OPEN
COME IN

PUT DOWNS

Some businesses will do as much as they can to help you with a problem over something you have bought; others may claim that there is nothing they can do. Don't give up if the shop tries to get out of its legal obligations…

…we'll send it back to the workshop

Only if you want them to. If you act reasonably quickly you can choose whether to ask for a full or partial refund, compensation, or to have the goods repaired or replaced (if that is a practical option). If the goods have developed a fault in the first six months it is assumed they were faulty when you bought them (unless the shop can prove otherwise).

… you'll have to take it up with the manufacturer

Wrong. You bought the goods from the shop and your contract was with them, not with a manufacturer who may be located on the other side of the world. If the goods genuinely don't work, the shop has not kept its side of the contract and you have a right to your money back. Shops normally have to accept responsibility for the manufacturer's claims. If the shop refuses to help, you can also use the guarantee to bring a claim against the manufacturer.

…we'll give you a credit note

No. If the goods are faulty, you're entitled to your money back. You don't have to accept a credit note if you don't want to. If you do accept a credit note, check where and when you can use it – some credit notes must be used within a fixed time and only in exchange for certain goods or services.

…sorry, it's out of guarantee

This can be tricky. A major problem with an expensive computer three months after the guarantee has run out can lead to a large repair bill. Raise the matter with the dealer and ask to talk to the manager. Use any documentation you have, such as manufacturer's literature, or details from their website,

We'll send it back to the workshop

Sorry it's out of guarantee

GUARANTEE ran out yesterday

use the law with care **try talking first**

You'll have to take it up with the manufacturer

...stressing the reliability and quality of the product, to show that it is not reasonable to expect a failure after such a short period. There's no hard and fast law about what is reasonable in terms of a product failure. It all depends on the circumstances.

...we don't give refunds on sale goods

Wrong. Unless the fault was pointed out to you or was something you should have seen when you bought them, goods bought in sales carry all the legal protection described above.

...we'll give you a replacement

Only if that's what you want.

We'll give you a replacement

However, if by now the fault has led you to decide that you don't really want the product after all, you are entitled to your money back - not a replacement. It's up to you to choose what to do.

Not satisfied If you are not satisfied with something that you have bought...

> Stop using it straightaway and take it back, with the receipt and guarantee (if you have one), to the shop where you bought it. It strengthens your case if you can do this as soon as possible. Your contract was with the shop, not the manufacturer, so it is the shop's responsibility to deal with your complaint. Even if you have lost the receipt, the contract still exists.

> Think about your legal position. Don't be afraid to use the law when making your case.

> Decide what you are going to say and what you would like the shop to do. Do you want your money back, or will you accept a repair or a replacement item?

> If the shop assistant doesn't help, ask to speak to someone more senior.

> Keep copies of all letters; if you talk on the phone, ask for the name of the person you are speaking to, and make a brief note of the conversation

> If you paid for the goods by credit card (and they cost more than £100.00), the credit card company, as well as the supplier, can be held liable for any fault. If the supplier does not deal with the problem properly, make your case in exactly the same way to the credit card company. You can also claim through the credit card company if the supplier has gone bust and is unable to deal with your claim.

The small claims court

If you cannot get any satisfaction over a problem with faulty goods or poor service, you can write to the person concerned warning them that you will try to recover the money they owe you by taking your case to the small claims court (strictly known as the small claims procedure in the Sheriff Court). You need to be 16 or over to do this; younger people need to ask their parent or guardian to bring the case on their behalf.

The small claims court is a simplified way of settling disputes where the value of the claim is less than £3,000. If the value of your claim is between £3,000 and £5,000, summary cause procedure can be used. When either small claims or summary cause procedure is used, a judge can hear your case without the expense of having to instruct your own lawyer. More details are available from your local Sheriff Court (under Courts in the phone book or at www.scotcourts.gov.uk), a Citizens Advice Bureau, or consumer advice centre.

Buying over the phone or on the internet

If you buy goods online or over the phone, your basic legal rights are the same as buying something in a shop. However, you also have a number of additional rights. These include the right to:

- **be given clear information about the nature of the product, what it will cost (including taxes and delivery), and the name and address of the seller;**
- **cancel your order up to seven days after you have received the goods (see below);**
- **have the goods delivered within 30 days of your order, unless you agreed with the seller that it would take longer. If the goods do not arrive within this time, you are entitled to a full refund.**

Cancellation

The above rights to cancel do not apply to certain goods and services, including food and other perishable items, unsealed computer software, CDs and DVDs etc, magazines, newspapers, and

use the law with care **try talking first**

tickets for travel, accommodation and events. For further details contact your local Citizens Advice Bureau.

Buying goods from outside the UK

If you buy goods from a country within the European Union (EU), your basic legal rights should generally be the same as they are here. However, chasing up a supplier in another country may be less straightforward than in the UK. If you buy something from outside the EU, be aware that the law may be different, and that it may be more difficult to pursue a complaint.

Further protection is available if you buy the items by credit card, see page 60.

Junk mail and phone calls

Junk mail

If you want to cut down on the junk mail and calls you receive, you can register with the *Mailing and Telephone Preference Services*, see **contacts** for details.

Spam

Most spam offers are a scam. If the message looks doubtful, delete it, and don't click on the adverts. Under the *Privacy and Electronic Communication Regulations 2003*, UK businesses can send direct marketing messages by email only to existing customers and to those people who have agreed to let them do so.

However, a great deal of bulk spam is sent from outside the UK, and there is little that UK law can do to deal with this.

Banking

Don't open emails claiming to be from your bank or building society asking you to verify your account or log-in details. Your bank will never ask you to do this. You can report the scam to your bank or local trading standards office.

VIEW CART

banks and building societies

Although there is no minimum legal age for someone to have a bank account, most banks offer basic accounts to young people aged eleven and over. These provide a cash card which can be used at a bank machine to withdraw cash, and possibly a debit card that will work only if there is enough money in the account. A regular current account is normally available only if you are 18 or over (or 16 or 17 with a steady income or an adult who will act as guarantor).

WHY HAVE A BANK ACCOUNT?

- many employers will only pay wages directly into an account;
- an account is needed for a student loan;
- the money can earn interest;
- it offers an easy way to pay bills;
- cashing cheques can be difficult and expensive without a bank account.

CHOOSING A BANK OR BUILDING SOCIETY

You will probably want to know:
- whether it has a branch near you and offers telephone and online banking,
- whether there are convenient cash points,
- about services offered and charges,
- what interest is paid on the money in your account. There will be leaflets on this, or you can ask a member of staff; and
- about special offers for young people.

Don't be persuaded by offers of free gifts if the services and charges are not as good as those of other banks or building societies, and always read the small print.

There are two main types of accounts: current accounts and savings accounts.

Current accounts

A current account is the normal account for day-to-day transactions. You pay in money, such as your wages, salary or student loan, which you can draw out as you please. You'll receive a debit card to pay for goods in shops and online, and to take out cash. You may also be given a chequebook and (if you are 18 or over) a credit card.

You'll also receive a regular bank statement (through the post or online) showing your overall balance and what has been paid in and withdrawn from your account.

Cheques

Plans to phase out cheques have been withdrawn. Banks have promised to keep cheques as long as customers need them.

If you write or receive a cheque, make sure that it is correctly written – for the correct amount, signed and dated (not post-dated, ie in the future).

Pay the cheque into your account as soon as possible, as banks don't usually accept cheques that are more than six months old.

Strictly speaking it is an

offence to write a cheque if you know that there is not enough money in your account to cover it, unless you have permission from your bank to do so. You will almost certainly face a penalty charge if the bank refuses to honour your cheque.

Never keep your chequebook and debit card together. If you do, it makes it much easier for a thief to take money from your account.

Cash cards Your cash card enables you to take money out of your current account from a cash machine using a confidential personal identification number (PIN). Never keep this number with your card. If your PIN number or card is stolen, contact your bank immediately.

Debit cards Your debit card allows you to buy things without writing a cheque or using cash. There is no legal age limit for obtaining a debit card, but as a rule, banks tend to wait until their customers are 16 years old.

You can use a debit card to pay for goods over the telephone or online. Your account is automatically debited with the amount you have spent. However, it can take a while (sometimes a few days) for payments to show on your balance.

You can only go overdrawn with a debit card, if you have the bank's agreement, otherwise you will be charged a fee.

Pre-paid cards Pre-paid cards are used to pay for goods and services in exactly the same way as a debit, credit, or store card. However, unlike these other cards, you load money onto a pre-paid card before you shop, and top up the card when your funds run low.

In some ways, pre-paid cards are more secure than debit or credit cards and, as they don't provide credit, do not require a credit check. Charges for cards vary greatly; there is usually a small issue fee, along with a further charge each month, or when the card is topped up.

Savings accounts A savings account normally provides a higher rate of interest. Most do not come with a chequebook or plastic card, and some have restrictions on when you can withdraw your money. You will still be able to withdraw money if you really have to, but will probably lose some of the extra interest.

If you keep money in your savings account while you are overdrawn on your current account or have a loan, you may find the interest you pay on your overdraft or loan is higher than the interest you earn on your savings account.

What about tax on the interest I earn? Any interest you earn on bank or building society accounts is normally taxed at 20 per cent before you receive it. If your level of income means that you don't pay tax, you can either get the tax back or arrange to have the interest paid without the tax being deducted. Ask your bank for a claim form, or go online for form R85.

banks and building societies

ISAs

An ISA (Individual Savings Account) is a special type of savings account where the interest you earn is not taxed. If you are under 16, you can open a Junior ISA and invest up to £3,720 per year. The money invested must remain in the Junior ISA until you reach age 18, at which point the account will convert into an ISA. There are two different types of ISA: Cash ISAs and Stocks and Shares ISAs.

Cash ISAs are similar to regular savings accounts. You can choose either a fixed term Cash ISA where a higher rate of interest is paid in return for your money being held in the account for a certain period of time, or an instant access Cash ISA where you can access your money at any time. You can invest up to £5,760 per year in a Cash ISA.

A Stocks and Shares ISA is where your ISA provider invests your money in stocks and shares. This type of ISA should usually only be used if you do not require access to your money for about five years. It is also important to remember that your ISA investments may go down as well as up, and therefore there is no guarantee that you will make a profit on your investments. You can invest up to £11,520 per year in a Stocks and Shares ISA. This amount is reduced by any amount saved in a Cash ISA in the same year.

credit

Credit is a way of buying goods by delaying the payment, or by paying in instalments. Credit cards and store cards are two forms of credit.

Credit cards You normally need to be at least 18 before you can have a credit card. Like debit cards, credit cards allow you to buy goods and services from shops, over the phone, or online.

Payment by credit card enables the shop to be paid straightaway (at a small cost to the retailer), and the customer to be billed sometime later. The person using the credit card is, in effect, being lent the money to buy the goods by the company issuing the card.

If you apply for a credit card, the credit card company will check your creditworthiness, a spending limit will be set on the account, and a fee charged if you go over this.

Each month you will receive a

statement showing how much you have spent, how much is owed, and the minimum amount you must pay. If you pay the bill in full, you will not be charged interest; however, interest will be added to your account if you do not pay off all the money that you owe.

If you make no payment at all, you will be charged a further penalty, your card may be cancelled, and your credit rating will suffer.

You can compare the cost of different cards by looking at the Annual Percentage Rate (APR) – the rate of interest charged by the firm issuing the credit card. The lower the APR, the lower the cost of borrowing

Store cards Store cards offer you credit when you buy goods at a particular store. You receive a regular statement showing how much you have spent, and what you owe. You are required to pay at least a fixed minimum amount each month, with the rest being carried forward and appearing on your next statement. Interest is charged on the amount you haven't paid off. These charges are often higher than other types of credit card. Details of the APR will be given on the store's website.

borrowing

Borrowing from a bank or building society A bank or building society lends money either through allowing an overdraft or by making a loan.

Overdrafts A person becomes overdrawn when they spend more money than they have in their bank account. If you need to go overdrawn, you can usually arrange an authorised overdraft with your bank, up to an agreed amount. Interest may be charged.

The most expensive overdraft is an unauthorised one – which is run up without the agreement of the bank. Interest is paid on the amount overdrawn, and charges are added on top of this.

If you ever find yourself in this situation, it is important to get in touch with the bank as soon as you can. Students may be offered interest-free overdrafts.

STATEMENT
60.00
10.00
44.00
-82.00
-23.78
-10.75
-23.78
6.31

borrowing

LOANS

A loan is an arrangement with your bank - or other financial institution - under which you are lent a specific amount of money. You enter into a contract for the loan. This will be at an agreed rate of interest and for a set period of time, during which you repay the full loan. If you are under 18 it is very unlikely that you will be able to get a bank loan, as these kinds of contracts with "minors" are not usually binding.

All loans are different. Always check the small print to see what you are signing up to.

PAYDAY LOANS

These are short term loans, available online and from high street shops, carrying very very high rates of interest. The loan and interest charges are generally repaid within the next month, but borrowers face further heavy charges if they fail to repay the loan in full within the agreed time.

Payday loan companies are not allowed to exert excessive pressure on borrowers (eg by harassing them on the phone), nor may they take money from a customer's bank account without the customer knowing about it or put pressure on them to borrow even more money.

If you are thinking about taking out a payday loan, seek informed impartial advice beforehand, see contacts.

Buying goods by instalments – credit or hire purchase

You can often buy more expensive goods (cars, computers, TVs) by instalments - that is, by paying only part of the price at the time of purchase, and paying the rest later.

Sometimes credit is available interest-free, but credit is normally an expensive way of paying for things. It is always a good idea to check the charge (the APR) that is being made.

Hire purchase is a special form of buying on credit. Technically the shop sells the goods to a finance company and you pay to "hire" them over an agreed period. When you have paid off what you owe you make a final payment to purchase the goods (hence "hire purchase"). Only then do you become the owner.

Second thoughts If you signed a credit deal at home (or away from the shop or business premises) you have a right to cancel if you act quickly. You will be sent a second copy of the agreement that will tell you how to cancel if you want to. You will usually have five days in which to do this.

getting into debt

People get into debt for all sorts of reasons. They may find they owe money to several different people and are tempted to borrow more to pay off some of these debts. This often becomes even more expensive.

You know it's getting serious when you start getting badgered to make repayments by the people you owe money to - your "creditors" - and you can't meet all the demands.

What to do

- **Don't ignore the problem:** it won't go away and will get worse the longer you leave it. You can get free help from a range of advice agencies.

- **Draw up a budget:** list all the money you owe and the people to whom it is owed; what your income and reasonable living expenses are; and see how much you can afford to pay back.

- **List your debts in their order of priority:** at the top are those where non-payment can have really serious consequences - like losing your home; having the electricity or gas cut off; or where non-payment is a criminal offence (like council tax and your TV licence). You should aim to pay these off first and then work out what's left over for the others, treating them equally.

- **Contact all your creditors:** go and see them or write or phone; explain the position and show them your budget. Discuss with them what you can reasonably pay. Usually they will be prepared to negotiate. You may be able to agree to pay by instalments or, for a period of time, just to pay off the interest on your loan. If you are worried about contacting them directly, get in touch with a free advice agency for help

- **Don't borrow more without getting advice:** some individuals and companies lend money at very high rates of interest, making it difficult to keep up with the payments and hard to keep out of debt.

HELP

You can get help and advice from experts. Try the National Debtline or a Citizens Advice Bureau, see contacts.

insurance

Insurance is a way of protecting yourself and your property from an unexpected loss or mishap. You can insure yourself against almost anything - losing your possessions in a fire, having them stolen or damaged, or having to face unexpected medical bills on holiday abroad. If you drive a car or motorcycle, you must be insured by law, see travel and transport, page 105.

In return for a premium - an agreed amount of money you pay each month or year - an insurance company will, if the worst does happen, pay you compensation for the losses or damage that you insured against (usually minus an excess that you have to pay yourself).

Buying insurance

There are two ways of obtaining insurance. You can either deal directly with the company, by phone or online, or go to a broker. Online comparison sites also enable you to compare the rates offered by different companies.

All the information you give should be accurate. Questions must be answered truthfully, and all other relevant information should also be given. If it's not, the insurance policy will be invalid and the insurer may refuse to pay your claim.

Keep a copy of any forms that you complete, and when you renew your insurance (usually done each year) don't forget to tell the insurance company about anything that has changed that might affect your insurance position. If you don't, again the policy may be invalid. Also, check the small print, so you get what you need included in your insurance.

use the law with care **try talking first**

THE WORDS THEY USE:

Broker
An agent who can help you choose and apply for insurance.

Cover
Insurance against loss or damage.

Cover note
A temporary document showing that you have insurance cover, usually sent out while the official certificate is being prepared.

Excess
The amount you will have to pay towards the cost of your claim. You can sometimes pay an extra payment – called a waiver - to reduce this

No claims bonus
The discount you are given on your premium if you haven't made a claim.

Policy
The document setting out the terms and conditions of your insurance.

Premium
The amount you pay for your insurance.

Quotation
A statement of the amount you will have to pay for the insurance you asked for.

tax

Income tax

Money paid in income tax is used to pay for services provided by the state - such as health, education, defence etc. Everyone who earns or receives income over a certain amount in a year pays income tax and, generally speaking, the more you earn, the more you pay. Current tax rates on income range from 20 to 45 per cent (2013).

As well as earnings from full and part-time work, tips and bonuses, tax is also paid on interest from savings with banks, building societies, and some National Savings accounts. Income tax may also be paid on pensions, income from savings and rent, and certain state benefits.

PAYE (Pay As You Earn) Your employer will usually take the tax from your earnings each time you are paid and pass the money on to the tax authorities, HM Revenue and Customs. Everyone is entitled to receive a certain amount of money on which they pay no tax at all. This is called a personal allowance, which, for a single person in 2013/14, is £9,440. Income tax is paid only when your income rises above this. There are other allowances which may be available, eg for the cost of tools or special clothing if they are not provided by your employer. If you are on a training programme, your grant in most cases is not taxable.

If you have been working and paying tax, but believe your total income for the year will be less than £9,440, contact HMRC and explain why you think you have paid too much tax to claim a refund.

Failure to complete your tax forms correctly can mean extra interest

payments and even fines. HMRC runs a telephone helpline, giving information and advice on tax, see **contacts**.

If you are a student with a holiday job, ask your employer for form P38(S) if you think your total taxable income for the year (including earnings and Income Support), will be less than the basic personal allowance, ie £9,440. Fill in the form, return it to your employer, and you should then be paid without tax being deducted

Tax credits Working Tax Credits and Child Tax Credits are available to those on low incomes to top up earnings. See the HMRC website for further details.

NATIONAL INSURANCE

Almost everybody in Britain who is in paid work must pay National Insurance contributions if they earn more than £146.00 per week. This money is used to help run the National Health Service and to provide pensions and benefits.

It is generally taken by your employer from the money that you earn. Everyone has their own NI number which they receive just before their 16th birthday. Your NI number is used to record all your NI contributions and must be given when claiming benefits.

family

INDIVIDUALS ENGAGING IN SOCIETY

Citizenship Foundation

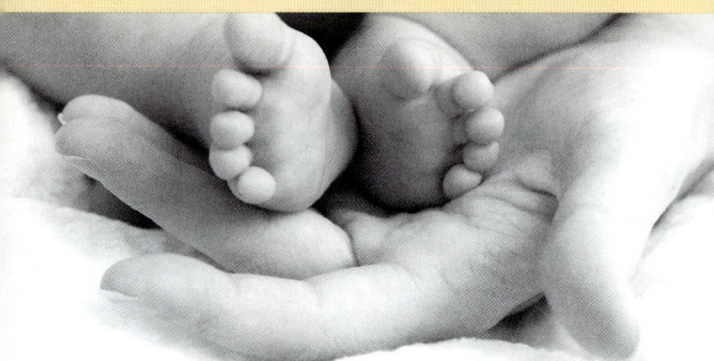

The birth and name of a child must be registered within 21 days of birth. This may be done at any registration office in Scotland.

If the baby's parents are married, the birth may be registered by the mother or father, and both parents' details will be included.

If the parents are not married they generally need to sign the birth register together for both their details to be included. If the mother is not married to the father, she can choose to register the birth on her own, and the father's details will not be included.

Changing your name

Under 16

A child's name can be changed with the agreement of both parents, unless the child is in care. In this case the child's name cannot be changed without the agreement of the court or everyone with responsibility for the child. The child can also object by applying to court.

If one parent wants to change their child's name, but the other parent or the child objects - then the parent or the child can apply for a court order to prevent this. Courts are very reluctant to agree to change a child's name against their wishes because of the importance of a name to a child's sense of identity.

If you can produce evidence to the Registrar General that you have been using your new name for two years, your birth certificate may be changed to reflect this. You can obtain the relevant forms for this at any local registration office or write to National Records of Scotland, see **contacts**.

Over 16

You can call yourself what you like and, if you want to change your name, you can just go ahead and do so. But you can't change your name to mislead or defraud someone.

Although you are free to be known by whatever name you wish, it can be difficult to prove your identity if the name you use is not the same as the one on your birth certificate. The best way to confirm your new name is by a applying to the General Registrar at National Records of Scotland (see **contacts**) who will record this, provided the name has been used for a period of two years. Your local Citizens Advice Bureau or a solicitor can give you more information on this.

use the law with care try talking first

If you marry

Women often change their surname when they marry - but they don't have to. A woman can keep her own family name, or make a new one by joining her name with that of her husband.

A man can also change his name upon marriage to that of his wife with her agreement.

citizenship

Most of our legal rights and responsibilities arise just because we are living, working, studying etc in a particular place - in our case, the United Kingdom. This is citizenship in its widest sense.

Sometimes, however, people need to know which country they are legally connected to (or what their nationality is). Countries can base their rules on a number of questions, such as where the person was born, how long they have lived in the country and where their parents were born or live.

In brief Anyone born in the United Kingdom before 1st January 1983 is automatically a British citizen. British citizenship is also available to those born in the UK on or after this date as long as their parents were married and either parent was a British citizen and legally settled in the UK. If their parents were unmarried, British citizenship can only automatically be derived through their mother.

Since 2006, children born of unmarried parents can obtain British citizenship through either their mother or father, provided there is satisfactory evidence of paternity.

Becoming a British citizen by naturalisation or registration depends on a number of different factors, such as if you marry a British citizen, how long you have lived here, if you are permanently settled here (or intend to remain here permanently), and if you are of 'good character' and speak sufficient English.

This is a complicated process and you will need specialist advice. A solicitor or Citizens Advice Bureau can help you find this.

parents

How the law works

There are no laws that list the exact rights and duties of parents. It is impossible to write down everything a parent should do for a child.

Instead, the law states that all married parents and unmarried mothers automatically have parental responsibilities and rights (PRR) for their children. An unmarried father does not have automatic PRR for his child. He can obtain PRR by signing the birth register jointly with the mother, by making a formal agreement with her, by marrying her, or by being granted parental responsibilities and rights by the courts.

Parental responsibility and rights (PRR)

This means having the responsibility and authority to care for the child's physical, moral, and emotional needs. Parental rights are not free-standing rights – they exist only to enable a parent to discharge her or his parental responsibilities.

When a child or young person is taken into care, PRR are given to the local authority, although parents do keep certain rights and responsibilities.

The law puts the interest of the child first. The powers that parents have to control their children are for the benefit of the child, not the parent. Those who deal with children in a legal setting, such as social workers, doctors and lawyers, must take careful note of what a child says, particularly when the child is able to understand all the issues involved.

Parental rights ends when the child reaches 16, although a parent remains responsible for providing direction and guidance until the child is 18. A parent's duty to provide financial support for a child continues beyond the age of 18 to 25, if the child is in full-time education or training.

Providing a home

Parents have a duty to look after and care for their children until they are 16. However, once someone reaches the age of 16 they can leave home without their parent's permission. The police and other authorities are unlikely to stop anyone leaving home, even against their parent's wishes, unless they are in some kind of danger, or are unable to look after themselves. A child who is in danger might be referred to the Children's Panel; see also **home**, page 79.

Discipline

Parents have the right and duty to discipline their child - and this can include smacking. But corporal punishment must be "moderate and reasonable". If it is too harsh, parents risk prosecution or having their child's name put on the child protection register, or their child being taken into care. In several other European countries, it is illegal for a parent to strike a child and this is being considered in Scotland.

Education

Parents have a duty to make sure that their child has a suitable full-time education, between the ages of 5-16.

See **education**, pages 26 and 28.

BABYSITTING

Religion

Parents can decide the religion (if any) in which their child will be brought up. If they can't agree between themselves, they can go to court, where a judge will decide what is in the best interests of the child.

A court will listen to the views of the child concerned and these will be respected if the child clearly understands what is involved.

Medical treatment

In practice young people, aged 16 and over, can almost always agree to their own medical treatment without referring to their parents. However, in serious cases, a court may overrule a child's refusal to consent to medical treatment.

Before treating a young person under 16, however, a doctor will normally try to obtain the parent's permission unless it is an emergency or the young person is clearly able to understand what the treatment involves

There is no law giving the minimum age for a baby-sitter, nor one stating how old a child must be before it can be left alone. Parents must take all the circumstances into account. For example, the age of the baby-sitter, the availability of the parent(s), and the health of the children being looked after, count as relevant factors.

Parents have a legal duty to care for their children, and even when the child is with a babysitter, the parent still has responsibility for their care and safety. This means that parents must choose a baby-sitter who is able to look after their children properly. If a serious accident occurs while they are out, the parents may have to convince a court that they had done all that they could to make sure their child was being looked after properly. A baby-sitter under 16 will probably be thought too young to deal with an emergency.

adoption

Anyone who is under 18, and has never been married, can be adopted. A couple or an individual wishing to adopt a child must usually be at least 21. If a married couple wish to adopt, and one partner is the father or mother of the child, the parent need only be 18, but the step-parent must be at least 21. Since 2005, unmarried couples (including gay and lesbian couples) have also been able to adopt.

When children are adopted, they are treated in law almost as if they had been born to the couple or person who adopted them. Parents who adopt children are advised to be open about their child's birth family from the start, unless there are particularly strong reasons not to do so.

At 18, people who have been adopted have the right to see a copy of their original birth records, and can get more information from the agency that arranged their adoption. An interview with a counsellor to prepare them for this is available. For more information, see contacts.

living together

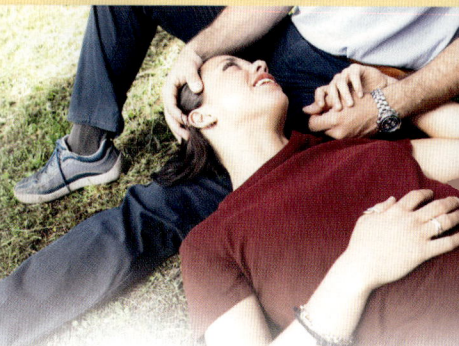

An increasing number of couples live together, sometimes with the thought of getting married later on, and sometimes not. Although this is a matter of personal choice, the law treats married and unmarried couples very differently.

Money and finance

A couple who live together without getting married are under no duty to look after one another, or to provide each other with financial support, unless it is something they have specifically agreed to do.

When children are involved, both parents, whether married or unmarried, have a legal obligation to look after them and provide for them until they reach the age of 16, or even later if they remain in full-time education.

If a married person dies without making a will, their husband or wife is entitled to most of their property. However, if they were not married, the surviving partner has to apply to the court in order to obtain any of the property, within six months of the death – a very short and strict time limit.

Children

Parents who are married share parental responsibility for their children. This means that both can make decisions about their children's upbringing. Unmarried fathers have this right if the couple have signed a formal parental responsibilities and rights agreement, or if the father has made a successful application to court for parental responsibility.

Home

Married couples have equal rights to occupy their home, whether they rent or own it, and whether or not it is in joint names. This continues even if their marriage fails, unless a court orders otherwise.

Unmarried couples do not have this right. If the home is in just one person's name, the non-owner may not have any automatic right to occupy the property and will have to apply to the court. However, non-owners can obtain rights over the value of the house if they make mortgage payments or improvements to the structure of the property. Couples can avoid difficulties caused by this by using a solicitor to write a formal contract setting out what would happen to their house and contents etc should the relationship come to an end.

 **Breaking up** Unlike a married couple, people who live together can end their relationship anytime they choose, without having to go to court.

Getting married

Legally, no one can be forced to marry against their wishes, and each partner must be 16 or over and unmarried. Marriages involving someone aged 15 or under are not recognised in law. In June 2013, a Bill making provision for same-sex marriage in Scotland began its passage through the Scottish Parliament.

In Scotland, under the *Marriages (Scotland) Act 1977*, you must obtain a marriage schedule from the District Registrar in the district where you live. You can then be married in a religious ceremony provided it is a religion authorised under the *Marriages (Scotland) Act 1977* or you can marry in a civil ceremony at a registration office.

Being married to more than one person at the same time - called bigamy - is normally a crime. But the marriages are recognised in Scotland if they took place in a country that allows marriages of this kind, and if each partner was legally free to marry in that way.

Civil partnerships

The *Civil Partnership Act 2004* allows same-sex couples, aged 16 and over, to register their partnership in a similar way to a civil marriage, and gives same-sex couples the same rights as people who marry. If either partner wishes to end the partnership, a formal court process takes place, through which the partnership becomes dissolved.

In July 2012, the Scottish Government set out its plans to legalise same-sex marriage.

VIOLENCE

A court can make an order, called an interdict, to protect a victim of domestic violence and can order one partner to leave the home for the other's protection - even if they are married. It is important for anyone in this situation to get advice from a solicitor as soon as possible.

divorce

A couple, who no longer wish to live together, can either end their marriage by divorce, or separate, keeping the marriage legally alive.

A separation may simply mean living apart, or it can be made more formal through a court order, known as judicial separation.

When one or both partners decide to divorce, an application is made to the local Sheriff Court or the Court of Session. It is usually made through a solicitor, but can be done by one of the partners alone.

If both partners can agree over their finances and together make satisfactory plans for the care of their children, it will probably not be necessary for either to appear in court. Nor is there likely to be any publicity in the papers

When the judge is satisfied that the appropriate arrangements have been made, that all the information is correct and that the marriage has broken down and cannot be saved, he or she will grant a decree of divorce. When this is granted, the marriage comes to an end.

Grounds for divorce

A person who applies for a divorce must prove to the court that their marriage has irretrievably broken down and that one of the following four things has happened:

1. the other partner has committed adultery, ie had heterosexual sexual intercourse with another man or woman and it is intolerable to live together;

2. the other partner has behaved unreasonably. This covers many things, including assault, refusing to have children, being excessively dirty or anti-social;

3. they have lived apart for one year, they both want a divorce, and are able to agree about on-going arrangements over their children and finances;

4. they have lived apart for two years.

but i had a bath last year!

Children

Parents going through a divorce are encouraged to reach an agreement between themselves over where their children will live and how often they will see each parent. But the judge will accept these arrangements only if satisfied that they are in the best interests of the child. If the child is felt to be old enough to have a view of their own, the judge will take the child's views into account.

Parents who cannot agree over this are often advised not to go straight to court (expensive and stressful for all concerned), but to negotiate reasonably in the best interests of the children. A court will, however, have to approve the final arrangements over children and money. It's usually felt to be in the children's interest to keep in touch with their family, so a judge will rarely stop a parent from seeing a child at all.

After the divorce, both parents normally keep parental responsibilities and rights over their child, and each should consult the other over decisions affecting their child's life, such as education, medical treatment, and religious upbringing.

Step-parents Step-parents do not have parental responsibilities and rights for their stepchildren, but the courts can require them to support a step-child. With their new partner, the step-parent may help with day-to-day things affecting the child, but major decisions should be taken by the child's birth mother and father - or only the mother, if they were not married (unless the father has parental responsibility).

Grandparents When a marriage ends, it may mean that a child is prevented from seeing other family members, such as grandparents, adding to the child's loss.

In this situation, grandparents can apply to a court for permission to carry on seeing the child or to have the child stay with them - although this can be more difficult to obtain than for parents.

Family disputes Sometimes parents become involved in legal disputes which directly affect their children - especially if they are getting divorced and cannot agree who the children should live with. In really important cases a young person who shows enough understanding of the issues, can act on their own initiative to instruct a solicitor and even make an application to the Court.

home

INDIVIDUALS ENGAGING IN SOCIETY

CitizenshipFoundation

a place of your own

Where do I look?

Advertisements for accommodation are found online, in local newspapers, supermarkets and the student union, if you are at college. The local council housing advice centre can tell you whether you are likely to qualify for council housing, and can also give you details of local housing associations.

You can also try solicitors' offices, estate agents and accommodation agencies. These agencies are not allowed, by law, to charge you for information about housing or lists of vacancies. Don't agree to pay them a fee. Normally they are paid for their services by the landlord. If you are asked for money and have any doubts, check first with the local Citizens Advice Bureau or Shelterline, see **contacts**.

You can own a house if you are over 16, but standard practice with banks and building societies is not to grant mortgages if you are under 18. You may also find it difficult to take on a private tenancy until you are 18.

What's the rent?

What does it include? How much is payable in advance? (Rent paid in advance will be lost if you leave without giving the right amount of notice.)

Your rent is fixed at whatever rate you agreed with your landlord. If you think the rent demanded is too high you can ask the rent assessment committee to decide what is reasonable for the property (ring your local council, or look under 'rent officer' in the phone book). If you are a short assured tenant (most are), you must do this within the first six months of the tenancy. There is no charge for this, but the committee can assess your rent only if there are enough similar flats or houses being let in the area.

The rate fixed by the rent assessment committee applies for at least twelve months from the date the rent was fixed, and a tenant can make only one application to the committee. It's a good idea to take advice before you do this, as your landlord may try to evict you. Sometimes the committee can put the rent up as well as down.

Do I pay a deposit?

This is an amount (often equal to a

HOUSING BENEFIT

If you are on a training programme, Income Support or a low wage, you may qualify for Housing Benefit from your local council. Your local housing advice centre or Citizens Advice Bureau can help you work out what you're entitled to. Housing Benefit is not available to full-time students, unless they have children or have a disability.

Discrimination

A landlord must not discriminate against a would-be tenant on grounds of sex, race, religion, disability, belief, or sexuality. There are a limited number of exceptions to this rule, particularly when the living space is shared with the landlord or his/her family. However discrimination on grounds of race, ethnic or national origin is not allowed under any circumstances.

Landlords also have a duty to make reasonable adjustments to accommodate

use the law with care **try talking first**

month's rent) paid to the landlord, or the agent, at the start of the tenancy. Always ask for a receipt when you hand over your deposit.

Landlords are now required to transfer all money held as a deposit to an approved Scheme Provider within 30 working days of receipt. The Scheme safeguards the deposit during the period of the tenancy.

If the landlord wishes to deduct money from the deposit to cover unpaid rent or bills, or repairs from damage you have caused, he or she must first contact the Scheme.

Any disputes between you and the landlord regarding the deposit can be settled by the Scheme.

Is there a service charge? This is money paid to look after the building and clean those parts that are shared, such as the stairs and corridors in a block of flats. If you rent your home from a private landlord or a housing association and pay a variable service charge as well as rent, you have the right to ask the landlord exactly how the service charge is calculated.

Do I need references? If so, choose people who have known you for a reasonable length of time, but preferably not a close relative. It is important to ask the person concerned first.

Your landlord or their agent is not allowed to charge you a referencing fee to secure the accommodation. It is unlawful, and you are not obliged to pay. If you have already been charged a fee, you are entitled to reclaim. Your local Citizens Advice Bureau should be able to help.

How safe? Landlords must, by law, have all gas appliances checked each year and must get a certificate of safety that you are entitled to see.

They also have duties with regards to electrical safety, such as annual PAT testing of electrical goods they have supplied and a five-year check of electrical installations. Landlords must also ensure that all smoke alarms installed after 2007 are mains-powered.

disabled people, although this is not normally required if landlord and tenant share the same property.

Leaving home If you are 16 or 17 and homeless, or feel that you can no longer live at home because you are being hurt, or because life at home is so bad, you can get help from social services.

Under the *Housing (Scotland) Act 1987*, local authorities must provide accommodation for homeless 16 and 17-year-olds who are in need, or whose welfare would be endangered if accommodation were not provided. However, some local authorities find it difficult to get hold of suitable accommodation for young people, and Income Support is not available to all 16 or 17-year-olds. Therefore, if you can, get advice from a housing advice centre or Citizens Advice Bureau before you do anything.

In care If you are leaving care, your local social services have a legal duty to provide help and advice.

tenancy agreements

If you rent a house from a local authority or housing association landlord you will probably have a **Scottish secure tenancy. If you are renting from a private landlord your tenancy will most likely be a short assured tenancy.**

Scottish secure tenancies

Under this arrangement you are entitled to remain in the property generally for as long as you wish, as long as you keep to the terms of your tenancy. If you don't, your landlord can obtain a court order to evict you.

Otherwise, you will only be required to leave in quite unusual circumstances; for example, if the house had to be demolished; in which case the landlord would be expected to find you suitable alternative accommodation.

Short assured tenancies

If you are renting from a private landlord, you will probably have a short assured tenancy, which is normally for a minimum of six months or one year, but can be longer.

Once your tenancy has come to an end, the landlord is entitled to try to have you evicted, provided he or she has gone through the correct procedures at the beginning and end of the tenancy.

REMEMBER With any type of tenancy agreement, a number of points should be borne in mind:

- If you are a tenant of a council or housing association, you will probably have the right to stay in the house as long as you want, provided you keep to the terms of the tenancy. If you are with a private landlord, your rights will be more restricted.
- It is generally a criminal offence for a landlord to evict a tenant without obtaining a court order. If this occurs, the tenant is also normally entitled to damages.
- If your landlord wishes to evict you because you have fallen behind with the rent, generally a court still has to be satisfied that it is reasonable to do so. However, if you are a tenant with a private sector landlord and still owe more than three months' rent at the time of the hearing, the court will generally have to grant an eviction order.
- You cannot leave before the end of your tenancy without giving the notice required in your agreement. If you do, your will be required to pay the balance of your rent, unless there is a "break clause" in your tenancy allowing you to leave early by giving an agreed period of notice. You can ask for this to be included in your agreement. (You don't need to do this with Scottish secure tenancy since these generally require only one month's notice).
- You have a right to receive from your landlord a written statement of the terms of your tenancy. This includes the date

that the tenancy began, the date that it ends, the amount of rent payable, and the date that it is due.

- Your landlord must give you formal notice to leave before taking any court action. If you are in this position, it is always a good idea to take advice from Shelter (see contacts), a housing advice centre, or a housing lawyer.

- If no action is taken by either side to end the tenancy, the tenancy will continue after the termination date set out in the lease. The amount of time it will continue generally depends on what is stated in the agreement.

- If you take the joint tenancy of a property with someone else, you are both responsible for making sure that you keep to the terms of the agreement. If one of you leaves before the end of the agreement, the other becomes responsible for the full rent.

Summary If you're a tenant of a council or a housing association, you will probably have a right to stay in the house as long as you want, provided you keep to the terms of your tenancy. If, however, you are with a private landlord, your rights will be more restricted. It is a complicated area of law. If there is any attempt to get you to leave, take advice. Often, what may seem a hopeless situation can be resolved in such a way as to allow you to stay, or at least give you a reasonable time before you have to leave.

Lodgings and hostels You do not have the same rights if you are in lodgings or if your landlord lives with you in the same house and shares the basic services with you. Your landlord only needs to give you "reasonable notice" and may not need to apply to a court to have you evicted.

If you are in hostel accommodation with a local council or housing association, they will not generally need a court order to evict you. They can give you notice at any time, as long as they keep to the terms of the hostel agreement.

Council tenants You have certain rights as a council tenant, which include staying in your house for as long as you want (assuming you pay your rent and do what your tenancy agreement says), taking in lodgers, and being consulted about the running of the estate. The council has a right to take action against tenants who cause a nuisance to others on the estate. In serious cases this has led to tenants losing their homes.

tenancy agreements

Repairs and maintenance

Who is responsible?

Your landlord is responsible by law for looking after the structure of the building, including outside fittings (such as gutters) and essential services (heating appliances not cookers - sinks, baths and toilets and the water, gas and electricity supplies). The landlord is also responsible for any other repairs that are necessary to keep the house in a habitable condition. Tenants are responsible for repairs for damage that they or their visitors cause, but not for fair "wear and tear". Repairs have to be done within a reasonable period.

Dear Landlord
As I explained to you by (phone/letter) on (date), the water heater at (the address) is broken and, although it is your responsibility to put this right under our tenancy agreement, it has not been fixed.
Therefore, I have obtained (three) estimates for repairs from (names and addresses of firms), which I enclose.
Unless I hear from you by (date) that you will do these repairs straightaway, I will have no option but to ask (name your choice) to do the repair. I shall then deduct their bill from future rental payments.
Yours sincerely,

Getting them done

Tell the landlord when the repairs need doing - and keep paying the rent. If the landlord does nothing and the problem concerns serious questions of health and safety, you can get in touch with the local environmental health office. They have the powers to get something done, and can make the landlord carry out the necessary work. Their number is in the phone book or online, under the name of your local council.

If the problem is less serious, or the environmental health department won't take action, and you are sure that the landlord is responsible for doing the repairs and has failed to do them within a reasonable period, write to the landlord explaining you intend to undertake the work yourself, sending three estimates of the cost. Give your landlord some time to consider the letter. If the landlord still fails to do the repairs you may go ahead with them yourself, taking the cost from your rent. Keep detailed records of everything you've done and a copy of every letter you write and receive.

If you ask in writing for repairs to be done, and your landlord fails to do them,

you can also complain to the Private Rented Housing Panel, see **contacts**.

Eviction

Generally speaking, you cannot be made to leave the house or flat that you are renting, unless the landlord has given you notice in the correct way and obtained a possession order from a court. In most cases, it is a criminal offence for anyone to evict you without a court order, or to try to force you out with threats. A court order may not be necessary, however, if you live in lodgings, or your landlord lives on the premises.

If you're threatened with eviction, get advice straightaway from a solicitor, local council housing department or Citizens Advice Bureau. Make sure you keep on paying the rent. Failure to pay will make it easier for the landlord to require you to leave.

use the law with care try talking first

Harassment

Your landlord is not allowed to use violence or threats of violence to force you to leave. This is a criminal offence. If you are assaulted or threatened, call the police.

If your landlord behaves in a way designed to make you leave - like changing the locks, shouting abuse or playing loud music – he or she will be breaking the *Rent (Scotland) Act 1984* and the *Housing (Scotland) Act 1987*. Again your local council, housing advice centre or Citizens Advice Bureau can help.

■ BRIEF CASE: Laurie

A few weeks after signing a six-month tenancy agreement for a bed-sit, Laurie was told to leave. His landlord had decided to sell the house and knew he would get more money for it with Laurie out of his room. The lock on Laurie's door was taken off, and the landlord threatened to tip his possessions into a black plastic bag. Without a job, Laurie spent more than two months sleeping in his car. With legal advice, and using legal aid, he took his case to court. The judge decided Laurie had been illegally evicted and ordered the landlord to pay him £36,500 in compensation - the extra amount of money the landlord made by selling his house without a tenant.

Insurance

If you are living in rented accommodation, insurance for the building is normally arranged by the owner. However, buildings insurance will not cover the cost of replacing your things if they are damaged or stolen. You can arrange to insure your belongings through an insurance company or a broker; see money, page 64.

If you have anything of particular value, you will need to list it separately on the insurance and find out exactly how much it costs to replace. The same applies to something like a bike that may be stolen or lost outside the home.

Some policies will give you the full replacement cost; others take into account wear and tear, and pay you less. If you are under-insured it means that your belongings are insured for less than their real value. If the insurance company discovers this when you make a claim, the amount they pay out is likely to be reduced.

Noisy neighbours

The best way to tackle a problem of noise, or any other nuisance, is to talk to the person concerned, if possible, before the situation gets out of hand. Sometimes this is easier and more effective if several people complain together. If this doesn't work, write a simple letter (keep a copy), and allow a reasonable time for your neighbour to respond.

If that fails, get in touch with your local environmental health department, whose staff have powers to investigate and deal with the matter. See also **leisure**, page 93.

homelessness

Council help If you are homeless, the council housing department should be able to help. It has a legal duty to give you advice and help towards finding somewhere to live, but this is not the same as offering you somewhere to stay. The council has to house you only if you are 16 or over and:

- **homeless, and**
- **in priority need, and**
- **have a connection with the local area, and**
- **have not made yourself intentionally homeless.**

You should qualify as a priority need if:

- **you're pregnant, or**
- **you have a child who depends on you, or**
- **you've had to leave your last home because someone was violent towards you, or**
- **you've lost your home through something like a fire or flood, or**
- **your age, health problems or disability makes you vulnerable and unable to cope with being homeless, or**
- **you are 16 or 17.**

If you have recently left care you are entitled to suitable accommodation until you are 18. Seek advice from Shelter or other housing advice centres.

Sleeping rough This is dangerous, and places the person at risk of being assaulted. Without an address, it is harder to get a job and even benefit. Someone found sleeping rough or begging more than once may be fined.

SQUATTING

In England and Wales, a squatter is someone who enters and occupies land, or any part of a building, without the owner's permission. Squatting in residential buildings is a criminal offence in England and Wales and can lead to imprisonment, or a fine, or both. Squatting in a non-residential building is not a crime, but squatters may commit an offence if they cause damage when getting into the property or using gas or electricity without first making the proper arrangements.

In Scottish law, there is no equivalent of the so-called "squatters' rights" that exist in England and Wales. In Scotland, occupying a building without permission amounts to trespass, and reasonable force (perhaps involving the police) may be used to remove those involved. Often a court order is obtained first; and this can be done very quickly.

CONTACTS see pages 146–153 for organisations able to give help & advice

going out

Not as planned

If you spend an evening at a match or concert looking at nothing more than a roof support or girder, then you have a right to complain and ask for a refund.

In fact, under the *Consumer Protection from Unfair Trading Regulations 2008*, it is a criminal offence for anyone selling or reselling tickets not to tell you about the location of your seat and anything that might spoil your enjoyment of the event.

There is no simple law setting out people's rights in the event of a change to the advertised programme or the cancellation of a performance. Your legal position will depend on such things as advance publicity, information given when the ticket was sold and the circumstances that forced a change of plan.

Although disgruntled spectators have been successful in taking promoters to court, legal action is not recommended for disappointment over a cancelled event. Some promoters will try to retain goodwill by offering tickets for another performance, or refunds. If they don't, it's worth explaining why you think their action is *unreasonable* - a key word in cases of this kind.

Hotels, pubs and off-licences

Licensing laws in Scotland are the responsibility of local Licensing Boards, that is, the licensing department within the local council.

Licensing Boards have wide discretion to decide the circumstances under which alcohol may or may not be sold; as a result, every pub and hotel has its own unique licence – with individual rules on things like access by children and young people. There is no over-arching rule on access to licensed premises by people under 18.

However, alcohol cannot be bought or consumed on licensed premises by someone under 18; although 16 or 17-year-olds accompanied by an adult are able to have beer or wine with a meal, as long as the alcohol is bought by the accompanying adult. Bar staff, however, retain the right to use their discretion and not serve a customer, as long as they are not breaking certain equality laws, see below. A licensee is under no obligation to explain their reason for refusing to serve alcohol.

The measures of alcohol that can be sold are legally controlled. A reasonable head forms part of a pint of beer, unless the glass has a line measure. The prices of drinks and food should be displayed by law, and should be clearly visible from where the drinks are served.

Drinks with 0.5% or less alcohol, such as some canned shandy and low alcohol beers, are treated as non-alcoholic.

use the law with care try talking first

CHALLENGE 25

It is an offence to sell alcohol to anyone under 18 - unless it can be shown that the landlord did their best to check the person was 18 or over. It's also an offence to buy, or to try to buy, alcohol if you are under 18, or to buy or try to buy it for someone under 18.

Licensed premises also have to observe a "Challenge 25" policy as a condition of their licence. This means that customers who look under 25 must be asked for ID. Failure to do this can lead to the bar losing its licence.

There are three forms of identification that licensees and their staff can accept as proof of age: a passport, a European Photocard Driving Licence, or an accredited proof of age card, see **contacts** for further details.

REFUSING TO SERVE

It is against the law for a pub or off-licence to refuse to serve someone because of their sex, religion, ethnic group, disability or sexual orientation.

However licensees may turn down customers who look as if they have had enough to drink already, otherwise they risk being charged with 'permitting drunkenness', and fined. Pub or bar staff may also refuse admittance to someone who appears to be intoxicated, or ask them to leave.

Not in public Under the *Confiscation of Alcohol (Young Persons) Act 1997*, a young person under 18 who has been drinking, (or is about to do so) in a public place (such as a street) or a place they have entered illegally, can be required by a police officer (or another accredited person) to stop drinking and surrender the alcohol. Refusal may lead to arrest or a fine of up to £500.00.

The officer can also take alcohol from someone over 18 who is in a public place, if they believe that the alcohol will be passed to under-age drinkers.

The police can ask for the name and address of anyone from whom they have taken alcohol in these circumstances, and it is an offence to refuse to give these details or to give a false name and address.

Increasingly across Scotland, it is against the law for anyone to drink alcohol on the street or in other public places.

Eating out

Quality

Whether you're in an expensive restaurant or an ordinary takeaway you have the right to reject any food of a quality below the standard that you are reasonably entitled to expect. What is 'reasonable' depends on such things as the price charged, what the menu says, and basic standards. The laws applying to faulty goods or services also apply to food. See **money**, pages 52-53.

Complaints

It's advisable to complain as soon as you know there's a problem, and before eating food you believe is unsatisfactory. The more you are paying the higher the standard you're entitled to expect.

If the quality of your meal is poor or the service is bad, you are entitled to make a reasonable deduction from the bill, but don't leave without paying. Explain to the manager why you are not satisfied, and leave your name and address. It is then up to the restaurant to take this up with you later on if they wish.

Price

Although there is no longer a specific legal requirement to display a price list, all restaurants, pubs and cafés must make sure that customers can easily access such information. In practice, this means that the price of food and drink can usually be found on a menu, blackboard, or notice before you order or sit down at a table.

Service charge

A service charge may sometimes be added to the bill in a restaurant. It is usually around ten per cent. If it was made clear before you ordered that service will be included, then you have to pay it. If the service was unsatisfactory, see the manager and ask for a discount. If there is no service charge included, it is up to you whether to leave a tip.

Safety

Under the *Food Safety Act 1990*, it is an offence for a restaurant to serve food that is unfit for human consumption. If you are concerned about the hygiene in a place where you have eaten, you can contact your local environmental health office, which has the power to investigate.

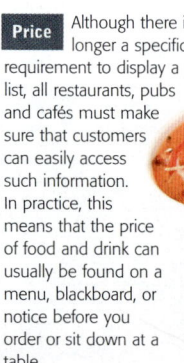

use the law with care try talking first

Raves

Anyone who organises a rave may need a public entertainment or alcohol licence. To get one, the event must meet certain safety standards. Many raves are legal and are arranged in conjunction with the local licensing authorities. Unlicensed raves are illegal.

Under the *Criminal Justice and Public Order Act 1994*, the police have the power to break up an unlicensed open air rave of more than 100 people if the noise and disturbance are likely to cause distress to local people. Under the direction of a senior police officer, the police can order off the land anyone who is preparing, waiting for, or attending the rave. They can also seize and confiscate any sound equipment. Anyone who goes back onto the land within seven days can be fined or imprisoned for up to three months. The police can also stop anyone within five miles of the rave, and order them not to proceed to the gathering. Anyone who refuses to turn back may be fined.

Although the police have the powers to close raves and unlicensed parties that break the law, they sometimes prefer to get involved only if there is a danger to people's safety or a serious nuisance.

Drugs Despite the drug culture that surrounds raves, the possession of drugs remains illegal and can lead to a criminal record, a fine and imprisonment.

Unlawful drugs can produce unpredictable and dangerous reactions – with severe mental and physical side effects. The use of ecstasy, for example, causes a rise in body temperature and an increased heart rate, giving rise to a danger of dehydration or heatstroke if body fluid is not replaced. Water is preferable to alcohol, as the latter dehydrates the body even further. For more information on drugs and the law, see **life**, page 9.

going out

GAMBLING

Under 18s are forbidden from going into a casino, betting shop, private club or adult gaming centre. They are also banned from gambling in alcohol licensed premises, for example, taking part in poker nights in pubs.

They are, however, allowed to play certain machines in some arcades, known as family entertainment centres.

Lottery tickets or scratch cards should not be sold to anyone under 16, and winnings cannot be collected by someone below this age.

If you're under 18, you are only allowed into a licensed bingo club if you don't take part.

Although it is accessible in the UK, online gambling is currently largely regulated from overseas.

Gambling contracts can be enforced in law. If the loser fails to pay, he or she can be taken to court.

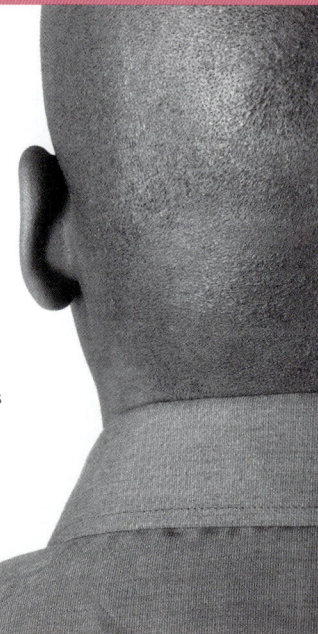

Nightclubs

Nightclubs in Scotland will have an alcohol licence, and do not normally require any other special licence. It is illegal for nightclubs, like pubs, to sell alcohol to someone under 18 or to someone who has already had too much to drink. Owners are within their rights to choose who they will or will not allow in - as long as they do not break the anti-discrimination laws. Clubs who charge lower entry fees for women than men are breaking the law.

The door

Door stewards, who act for the licensee, have the right to refuse entry — as long as it is not on the grounds of unfair discrimination, see page 87, and do not have to give reasons for their decision.

They may use only a reasonable amount of force to get someone to leave which, in certain circumstances, means no force at all.

Under the *Private Security Industry Act 2001*, all door supervisors must now be licensed. It is an offence for a supervisor or security guard to operate without one.

use the law with care try talking first

If you want to get home safely, use a licensed taxi or private hire car or the bus.

Black cabs, licensed taxis

These are under tight licensing control. The vehicles must be checked regularly, the fares are set by law, and the drivers may have had to sit an exam to get their licence.

Black cabs can be flagged down, as well as hired from a taxi rank. From a rank a taxi driver cannot unreasonably refuse to take a fare. It is a criminal offence for a driver of a cab to lengthen the journey in time or distance without a good reason.

Under equality legislation, newly licensed taxis in most areas have to be fully accessible to disabled travellers. Black cab and licensed taxi drivers are also required to help disabled people in and out of taxis and to help with their luggage - although drivers can claim exemption from these regulations if they have a back injury that prevents them from lifting heavy objects.

Private hire cars

All minicabs, private hire cars and their drivers must be licensed by the local authority. If you want a private hire car, you should either book it in advance or wait in the cab office. Even if there's a meter, it's a good idea to get an estimate of the fare before you set off. If there's not, always agree the fare in advance.

Unlicensed taxis and private hire cars

Unlike black cabs or licensed taxis, these vehicles have not been specially examined, and may not even have a current MOT. They will also not be insured to carry fare-paying passengers, so passengers have little protection if anything goes wrong.

No entry

The driver of a licensed taxi or hire car who, without good reason, refuses to take a passenger (including a disabled person) may be prosecuted and fined.

Anyone who feels that they are a victim of this, and wishes to do something about it, should make a note of the plate or registration number of the taxi or hire vehicle and report the matter to their local licensing authority, ie local council.

The licensing authority will investigate the case and prosecute the driver if they feel there is sufficient evidence of an offence.

staying in

Parties

Drink and drugs

Although you can't buy alcohol from an off-licence until you're 18, anyone over five can drink alcohol on private premises. It is an offence to give alcohol to a child under five, unless it is administered by a doctor or is in an emergency.

An offence is committed, under the *Misuse of Drugs Act 1971*, to knowingly allow anyone into your flat or house to supply an illegal drug to someone else, or to allow the smoking of cannabis. You can still be charged even if you are not taking the drug yourself, as it is your place they are using.

The penalty for allowing drug-taking on your premises is up to 14 years in prison for a Class A or B drug, and up to five years for a Class C drug. See also **life** page 9.

Safety

You invite some friends around for the evening and one of them falls down the stairs. If the cause of the accident was the state of the carpet rather than too much beer, you or your parents could be liable for their injuries. This doesn't mean wrapping every sharp corner in cotton wool, but something like a loose piece of stair carpet definitely should be fixed, since it is reasonable for visitors to expect to walk down the stairs safely. You're not expected to guard against the unforeseeable. If someone slides down the banisters and breaks a leg, then that's their problem.

Insurance

If someone is injured in your home you could be required to pay them compensation - although this can be paid through an insurance policy, if you have one. Most householders' insurance policies cover owners for injuries to other people called "third parties" caused by the state of the buildings or its fittings. If you're in rented

use the law with care try talking first

accommodation, your landlord could be liable - and again it is his or her insurance company that would pay damages. If you face this problem you can check with a solicitor or Citizens Advice Bureau.

Gatecrashing Gatecrashing is trespass. The law says that you can use reasonable force to get gatecrashers to leave, but don't start waving a broken bottle around. This is unreasonable and will leave you in more trouble than them.

Noise If there is a noisy party and the police are called, they can ask people to be quiet, but there's not much else they can do unless they fear there's going to be a breach of the peace - that is some kind of disorder. Then arrests will almost certainly be made.

However, if you are being disturbed by noise from a neighbour between

11.00pm and 7.00am, you can ring the local environmental health department, which must investigate your complaint as soon as possible.

Under the *Environmental Protection Act 1990*, they have the power to send an officer to the house to measure the noise and decide whether it is excessive. If it is, the person believed to be responsible will be given a warning notice, requiring the noise to be switched off or turned down within ten minutes. An offence is committed if the noise continues. The officer can decide to prosecute or issue an on the spot fine of £100.00.

If the warning notice is ignored, the officer can also obtain a warrant (often very quickly) to go into the building and remove the sound equipment that is being used.

For other problems with noisy neighbours, see **home**, page 83.

staying in

TV, videos, music, games and the internet

TV licence

A licence is required to watch or record TV as it is being broadcast – whether using a television, computer, laptop, mobile phone or DVD/video recorder. Watching TV without a licence is a criminal offence and can lead to a fine of up to £1,000. A licence is not need to watch catch-up services online.

One licence covers all the equipment in a single home. If rooms are rented separately, a licence must be obtained for the TV equipment in each room. Students living in a hall of residence with a TV in their room also need their own licence.

TV Licencing officers have no right of entry to your home without a search warrant.

Copying and recording

Strictly speaking, you can make a copy of a TV or radio broadcast for your own use, but only so you can view or listen to it at a more convenient time. It is against the law to record a programme if you intend to keep it as part of a collection or because you find it particularly interesting or enjoyable. Copying a CD, tape or computer game belonging to someone else is also illegal.

The internet

All music and recordings of music are copyrighted (that is, owned by someone) for at least 50 years from the date on which they were published or recorded.

Downloading music files (whether for personal use or profit) without permission from the copyright owner (the artist or record label) is illegal.

Pornography

Accessing pornography is, in general, not an offence, unless it involves a child – ie someone under the age of 18 – which is dealt with very strictly in law.

It is an offence to take, distribute, or possess an indecent photograph or image of a child. (An image may be moving or still, and includes graphic cartoons.)

It is also an offence, punishable by up to three years in prison, to possess or intentionally view on a computer material that shows extreme acts of violence or sexual interference.

■ BRIEF CASE: No excuse

A mother of a 14-year-old girl faced a bill of £4,000 to be paid in compensation for the music files that her daughter had illegally downloaded on the family computer. The mother stated that she herself was not computer literate and had no idea what her daughter had been doing.

use the law with care **try talking first**

Risks and the duty of care

Anyone who plays sport must expect to suffer the sorts of injuries normal to the game concerned. But intentional or reckless damage to someone else is another matter, and the player responsible can be sued for damages and prosecuted for a criminal offence.

Organisers of sporting events also have a duty to see that players, visitors, spectators and passers-by are reasonably safe.

BRIEF CASE: Golf

A golfer who was hit in the eye in 2007 by another player's ball on a golf course in Winchburgh, West Lothian was awarded almost £400,000 in damages in 2011 by the Court of session in Edinburgh. Anthony Phee lost the use of an eye when he was struck in the face by a ball hit offline from a nearby tee as he walked between holes. The court decided that the golfer whose ball hit Mr Phee was 70 per cent negligent as he should have waited to move out of site before striking the ball. The Court also decided that the golf club committee was 30 per cent liable for failing to provide proper safety signs warning golfers of a potential danger.

Alcohol

It's an offence to be drunk at a football or rugby match or to have alcoholic drinks in the ground or on the supporters' coach or train travelling to or from the event.

the open air

All land in the United Kingdom is owned by someone - private landowners, a local authority, government body (e.g. Ministry of Defence), or the Crown, (the Queen). *The Land Reform (Scotland) Act 2003* gives everyone access rights to cross land, or be in or on land, water or air for recreational or educational purposes, providing the right to be on land or water is exercised responsibly. This means that you can, for example, walk, swim or climb anywhere, as long as you do no harm to the landowner's property.

Footpaths If a route across a piece of land has been used for 20 years or more without interruption, that route may become a right of way. A right of way can be lost through disuse; however, this is less important now the rights of access to the countryside have been established. Strictly speaking, footpaths are for walkers only. It's a criminal offence to drive a motorbike or car on a path; however, some rights of way permit vehicular and other use.

Footpaths are shown on Ordnance Survey maps - but if you need to check on a path, you can ask to look at the maps in the local council planning office who may be able to give you information on the particular path, otherwise contact Scotways, see **contacts**.

The Land Reform (Scotland) Act 2003 has dramatically improved access to the countryside in Scotland. Your local authority will take action against any person putting up a misleading sign, such as "private" that discourages people from using a public right of way. If you come across a problem of this kind and want something done, contact the local council.

The local council's Rights of Way Officer has a duty to make sure that public rights of way are kept open and free from obstruction. It's the local council's responsibility to maintain footpaths so that people can walk along them, and the job of the landowner to look after stiles and gates along the path, footpath, or bridleway.

BULLS

Checking your legal rights here needs some farming knowledge and the ability to tell one breed of bull from another without getting too close. All dairy bulls (breeds like Friesian, Guernsey and Jersey) are banned from fields crossed by public paths. Other types of bull are allowed only if they are in with cows or heifers, which apparently makes them much less aggressive.

use the law with care **try talking first**

Fishing

You can fish in the sea and in tidal waters at any time, unless there are local by-laws forbidding it. All fishing rights in Scotland are owned, which means you need to pay for permission from the owner to fish. Some local authorities own fishing rights and permit residents to fish free, or for a nominal charge.

Beaches

Land between the low and high tide lines is the property of the Crown - but there is almost never a problem in walking along a beach. The *Land Reform (Scotland) Act 2003* gives powers to the public to access beaches providing they do no harm to the landlord's interests.

Pollution

The Scottish Environmental Protection Agency asks members of the public to report any environmental incident - on rivers, lakes, canals, or the coastline - or the dumping of rubbish, by contacting their local Scottish Environmental Protection Agency office, see **contacts**.

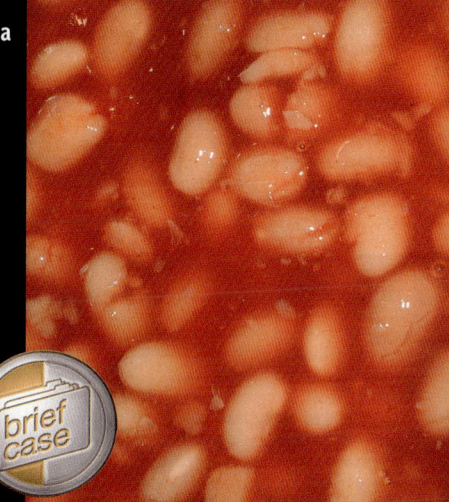

■ BRIEF CASE: Katrina

Katrina noticed that the water in the stream near her home was an unusual colour - particularly around the discharge pipe used by a local factory. She rang the Environment Agency who sent an officer to investigate. The officer reported that the water was discoloured and smelt foul and contained pieces of food that looked like shells from baked beans - which is just what they were. The company admitted polluting the river and was fined £5,000.

animals

Wildlife

The *Wildlife and Countryside Act 1981* protects a wide range of wild animals, birds and plants and covers killing, injuring, taking or possessing and disturbing their place of shelter or protection. The *Wild Mammals (Protection) Act 1996* makes it an offence to inflict unnecessary suffering on any wild mammal. The maximum penalty under both Acts is a fine up to £5,000 and/or six months' imprisonment.

Pets

Under the *Animal Welfare (Scotland) Act 2006* it is illegal to sell a pet to anyone below the age of 16, without the permission of that person's parent or carer. A pet owner has a legal responsibility to care for the animal and make sure it does not suffer unnecessarily. It is an offence to be cruel to the animal or to abandon it if it is likely to cause the animal unnecessary suffering.

Pet owners are also responsible for any damage their animal causes if they knew (or should have known) it was likely to cause such damage, or if their animal is defined as dangerous.

Dangerous animals are known, in law, as those that are not domesticated in this country that might be expected to have dangerous characteristics, such as a monkey or venomous snake. Anyone keeping an animal of this kind must have a licence.

Dogs

Under the *Control of Dogs Order 1992*, anyone owning a dog must make sure that it wears a collar with the name and address of its owner when it is in a public place. If a dog fouls any public place, eg a footpath or park, the person in charge of the dog commits an offence if he or she fails to clear up the mess.

It is an offence under the *Dangerous Dogs Act 1991*, to allow a dog to be dangerously out of control in a public place. The owner or person in charge of the dog can be fined or imprisoned for up to six months. The court can also order the dog to be destroyed, and can disqualify the owner from keeping a dog in the future. A farmer is allowed to shoot a dog that is not under anyone's control and is worrying livestock on their land.

Under the *Guard Dog Act 1975*, guard dogs should be under the control of a handler or else tied up and prevented from roaming freely. A warning notice should also be displayed. The Act does not apply to dogs guarding private houses or farmland.

■ BRIEF CASE: Abandoned

One morning, the SSPCA received an anonymous telephone call explaining that a dog had been abandoned in a house in a district just outside Glasgow. An SSPCA officer went to investigate and, with the help of the police, broke into the empty house, where they found a young retriever, with neither food nor water, and in a very distressed condition. The owner was traced and admitted the dog had been left alone for ten days. He was charged and found guilty of cruelty and abandonment, fined £150 and banned from keeping an animal for ten years.

travel
and transport

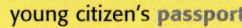

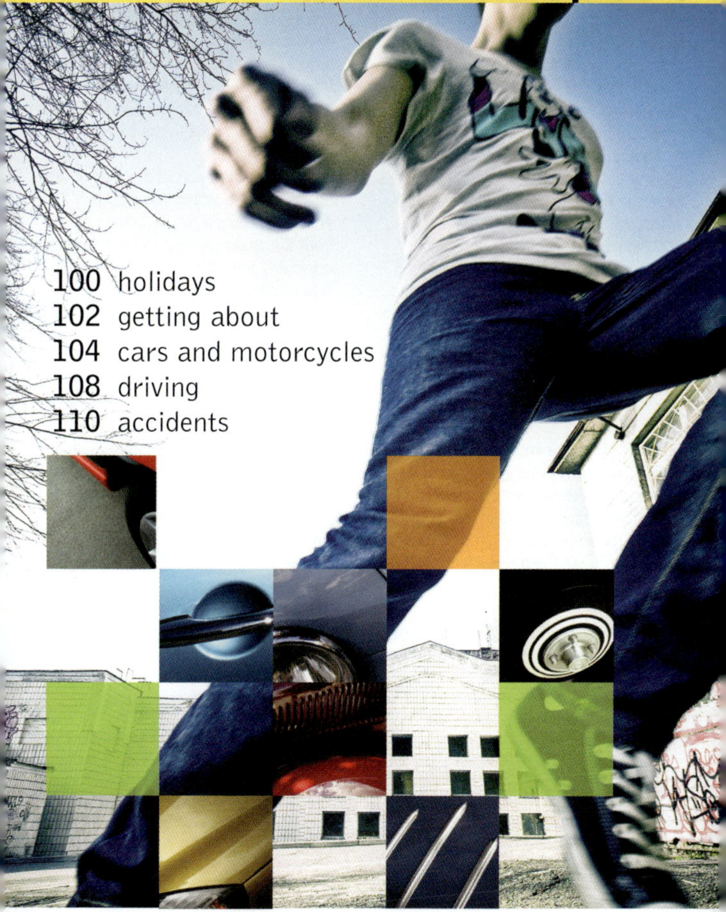

INDIVIDUALS ENGAGING IN SOCIETY

Citizenship Foundation

holidays

Package holidays

When you book a holiday, you are making a contract with the company responsible for arranging the package. This is usually the tour operator, but it can also be the travel agent, particularly if you have asked for extra arrangements to be made, not included in the brochure.

Although holiday brochures are designed to show the hotel or resort at its best, the *Package Travel, Package Holidays and Package Tours Regulations 1992* state that they must be accurate and not misleading. If the room or the swimming pool that you were promised is not available, you may be able to claim compensation because of the failure of the company arranging the holiday to keep its side of the contract.

It is an offence, under the *Trade Descriptions Act 1968*, for a firm to make a statement that it knows to be false about the goods or services it provides. Prosecutions for this are usually made by local trading standards officers.

If you have any special need, it's important to tell the travel agent or tour operator at the time you make the booking.

Before you sign or hand over any money, read the small print and check what it says about changes to your schedule. Under certain circumstances, travel organisers can alter flight times or accommodation arrangements provided they make this clear in the brochure or contract.

If you pay all or part of the cost of the holiday by credit card, you may be entitled to claim a full or partial refund from the credit card company if the firm organising the holiday fails to keep its side of the contract. For more information on paying by credit card, see **money** page 60.

If you are going abroad, it's also a good idea to book your holiday through a travel firm registered with ABTA, IATA or ATOL. These organisations cover the cost of getting you home, or compensating for your losses, if the travel company goes bust while you're away, or even before you've left. You'll find their symbol in the brochure or the holiday details online.

BEFORE YOU GO

- Check whether you need to have any vaccinations, and think about getting medical insurance, see below.
- If you are travelling in the European Union, or to Iceland, Liechtenstein, Norway, or Switzerland, get a European Health Insurance Card, and take it with you. It allows you free or reduced medical costs. Further information is available from post offices and the EHIC website, www.ehic.org.uk.
- Check your passport is up to date and whether you need a visa for the country you are visiting. British citizens do not need a passport to enter the Republic of Ireland - but some form of identification is required, such as a driver's licence or photo ID. If you have a passport, it's a good idea to take it with you.
- If you're thinking of hitching, check on advisability before you go. In some countries it is illegal. It always carries a risk.
- If you want to know more about travel requirements or conditions, look on www.gov.uk, *foreign travel advice*, ring the embassy of the country concerned, or visit the Foreign & Commonwealth Office website at www.fco.gov.uk, email: TravelAdvicePublicEnquiries@ fco.gov.uk, or tel 020 7008 1500.

use the law with care **try talking first**

TRAVEL AND MEDICAL INSURANCE

Travel insurance will protect you from losses while you're away, and even illness before you go.

Take the policy with you on holiday, so that if anything goes wrong you can make sure you keep to the terms of the agreement.

Passports Everyone who travels abroad, including young children, must have their own passport. Passport interviews are now required for everyone aged 16 or over when applying for a passport for the first time.

A passport for someone aged 16 and over costs £72.50. It is valid for ten years for travel to any country of the world. A passport for someone under 16 costs £46.00, and is valid for five years. More information is available from www.gov.uk or www.ips.gov.uk.

If something goes wrong If there is a problem with the holiday that the travel company has provided, tell them or their representative as soon as possible. Make a note of the facts and keep all evidence of extra costs. Photographic evidence may be helpful. If the problem is not resolved, contact the travel firm as soon as you get home.

If you're not satisfied with their reply, write to the managing director. If your complaint has not been properly dealt with, and the company belongs to ABTA, you can have your claim decided by an independent arbitrator, see **contacts**. It is also a good idea to seek advice as soon as possible from a Citizens Advice Bureau or, if necessary, a solicitor. Action through the courts should be a last resort.

If your luggage doesn't arrive, report the loss immediately. Try to obtain a copy of any reports you complete. Under international law, the airline is responsible for lost or damaged luggage, but compensation is paid by weight rather than value, and the airline will not be responsible for fragile items. It may be better to claim through your holiday insurance.

Lost or stolen If you lose all your cash and your cards, you can go to a bank and arrange for money to be transferred from home. There will probably be a charge, but the money should arrive within 24 hours.

If you lose anything valuable, tell the police and get a note from them confirming that you have done this. Contact the travel company if you lose your ticket home, and immediately report the loss of traveller's cheques or credit cards to the company offices. They often let you reverse the charges for the call. It is very important to report losses to your insurance company within the time limit stated in the policy.

If your passport is lost or stolen, contact the British Consulate who have an office in most big cities and should be able to provide you with help or advice.

In trouble Travellers overseas are automatically subject to the laws of the country they are visiting.

If you're arrested, insist on the British Consulate being informed. The Consulate will explain the local procedures, including access to a lawyer and the availability of legal aid. A European Union national can go to any EU Consulate, see **europe** page 140.

DELAYS

If your flight is delayed by more than three hours you may be entitled to compensation. The rules apply to all flights departing from airports in the European Union, and to those on EU-based airlines to airports in the EU. Compensation levels depend on the length of the flight and period of delay, see contacts.

holidays

Taking a vehicle abroad

A Green Card provides evidence of insurance. Although it is not strictly necessary for travel in the EU and certain non-EU states, it can be useful in the event of an accident, and is a requirement in a number of countries outside the EU.

You can check the requirements with a motoring organisation such as AA, RAC, and Green Flag, who can also advise you whether you need an International Driving Permit, and issue one, if required.

If you have an accident, tell the police and ask for a record or receipt. It will help with your insurance claim when you get home. For the same reason, it's also a good idea to take notes and photographs of the incident, including pictures of the number plates of the vehicles involved.

Don't sign anything in a language that you don't understand. If you're put under pressure, write "I don't understand" immediately above your signature.

Coming home

If you are returning from a country within the EU, you do not have to pay customs charges on any goods you bought in that country. There is generally no limit on the amount you can bring in – as long as the goods are for a gift or your own use.

Limits are, however, placed on alcohol and tobacco and anyone who exceeds these must convince the customs that the goods were not bought for commercial purposes, that is, to be sold on. No one under 17 is entitled to a tobacco or alcohol allowance.

Customs officials can check your baggage for prohibited goods or to see if you need to pay any tax or duty if you have been to a country outside the EU. Details of the powers and duties of customs officers are given on the Government website, www.gov.uk *passports, travel and living abroad*.

getting about

Public transport

Tickets

By the time you're 16, you generally have to pay full fare on all buses, trains, trams, and the Glasgow and London Underground. In some areas full fare is charged on buses from the age of 14.

If you travel on a train or the Underground without a ticket, you may be charged an on-the-spot penalty as well as the cost of your fare. Information about this is displayed in stations where this system is in operation.

If you are stranded at a station without any money for a ticket, your ticket can be bought for you by someone else at another station, with the authorisation sent by telephone to where you are waiting. This is known as a SILK – Stranded Individual Location Known – arrangement.

use the law with care try talking first

on UK coach fares. One year cards cost £10.00, and £25.00 buys a card valid for three years.

The Under 26 International Youth Travel Card provides members with discounted air fares worldwide, and also offers reductions on places to stay and visit. See **contacts**.

Some tickets are cheaper when travelling outside the rush hour, and travel cards give you further reductions. A 16-25 Railcard costs £30.00 or £70.00 for three years (2013 prices) and entitles you to a third off most rail ticket prices throughout Britain. Everyone aged 16-25 is eligible to have one, as are full-time students aged 26 and over. You can buy a Railcard at main stations, some travel agents, student services at college, by phone, or online, see contacts.

An InterRail Pass lets you travel by train at reduced rates in one or more European countries with discounts available on certain ferries. You must be a citizen of, or have lived, in Europe for at least six months and have a passport. InterRail cards are available from selected stations and travel agents, see also www.interrail.eu.

Young Person's Coachcards entitle young people aged 16-26 and full-time students aged over 26, to up to one third discount

COMPLAINTS

If your train (or bus) is late, there's not a lot in law that you can do about it. When you buy a ticket, you have no legal guarantee that the train will run on time (or even at all), or that you'll have a seat when it does come. All this is explained in the small print, known as the conditions of carriage, which can be checked at station ticket offices.

Under the rail company's Passenger's Charter, you may be offered a percentage of the ticket price in compensation if you're stuck on a train that has been seriously delayed, or if you have a season ticket for a train service that has been below the standard set for punctuality or reliability.

Complaints about a train service can usually be made on each rail company's website or on a complaints form available from a station on the route that you travelled.

■ BRIEF CASE: Emma

Emma bought a ticket for a day trip to Edinburgh, saying that she wanted to travel on the next train, leaving in 15 minutes. When the inspector checked her ticket on the train, she asked Emma to pay a further £6.00, as she had been undercharged by the booking clerk. Although Emma claimed that it was the train operating company's mistake in selling her the wrong ticket, by law she had to pay the difference. When a contract is made, one side cannot gain by the other side's genuine mistake.

Getting started

The licence

It is an offence to drive or ride a motor vehicle without the correct licence. You get a full driving licence when you have passed your test, and the licence will be valid until you are 70. Licences for drivers over 70 are issued for three years at a time.

A licence is now the size of a credit card and contains the holder's photograph. If your details, eg name or address change, you must tell the DVLA (see **contacts**) - or risk a fine.

If you want to learn to drive, you need a provisional driving licence. Application forms are available from post offices and online. When you get your licence, sign it immediately - don't drive until you have done so. Car drivers can hold the same provisional licence until they are 70, as can motorcyclists but their compulsory basic training certificate has to be renewed every two years.

Learning to drive a car

When you are driving on a provisional licence you must display 'L' plates, which should be removed or covered up when the vehicle is not being driven by a learner. You must not drive on a motorway, and you must have someone with you in the front passenger seat of the car who is over 21 and has held a full EU driving licence for at least three years. This person must be fit to drive and must not have had more than the legal amount of alcohol.

The driving test is in two parts: a two stage written theory exam, which costs £31.00; and a practical test, costing £62.00. The theory paper, which is taken online, must be passed before taking the practical test. For more information see the Government website, www.gov.uk, *driving, transport and travel*.

Learning to ride a motorcycle, moped or scooter

Motorcyclists also have to take a theory paper and a practical test to gain a licence, unless they already have a full car licence, when only the practical test is required. Before you can ride a motorcycle on the road, you are generally required to successfully complete a Compulsory Basic Training course. Once you have your CBT certificate you can go on to take the theory and practical tests to qualify for a full moped or motorcycle licence.

You can ride a moped on the road from the age of 16, but cannot take up a full moped licence until you are 17. This is also the minimum age for learning to ride a motorcycle, which must have an engine size no larger than 125 ccs and a maximum power output of 11 kw.

Learner motorcyclists may not ride on a motorway, nor carry a pillion passenger, unless the passenger is also licensed to ride that type of machine. Mopeds, scooters, and motorised skateboards cannot be used on the public roads without a licence, road tax, and insurance.

MOT

Most vehicles that are three or more years old must pass an MOT test if they are to be used or left on the road.

Road tax

A car or motorbike must display a current tax disc, whether it is being used or just standing on the road. The fine for breaking this regulation is normally about twice the cost of the disc. The Driving and Vehicle Licensing Agency, known as the DVLA, has powers to wheel clamp and remove vehicles not showing a current disc, and to charge a fee for their release. It is a crime to use a tax disc belonging to another vehicle.

If you take your vehicle off the road and decide not to tax it, you need to inform the DVLA and make a Statutory Off Road Notification (SORN), see **contacts**.

Insurance

It is an offence to drive, ride or even place, a motor vehicle on the road without insurance. The penalties for this are very heavy, and it makes no difference for someone to say it was a genuine mistake and that they thought they were insured. Failure to have insurance means a fine and penalty points on a licence, and possible disqualification.

It is also an offence for someone to allow their car or motorcycle to be used by a person who is not insured to drive it.

There are three different kinds of motor insurance, offering different levels of cover:

• **third party insurance only pays for damage caused to other people or their property (and not to your own vehicle). This is the minimum level of insurance cover required by law;**
• **third party fire and theft gives you**

further protection by covering your vehicle against theft or fire damage;
• **fully comprehensive insurance is usually the most expensive, but covers the cost of accident repair damage to your vehicle as well as compensating you and others for injuries or damage in the accident.**

When you apply for any insurance, make sure the information you give is accurate and complete. If it's not, your insurance will be invalid. It's an offence knowingly to make a false statement to obtain insurance. For more information, see **money**, page 64.

■ BRIEF CASE: Sarah

Sarah bought a Morgan sports car, and insured it for her and her fiancé to drive. The car, worth £26,000, was stolen. When she claimed on her insurance, it came to light that her fiancé had received a serious motoring conviction several years ago, which Sarah had failed to mention on the application form. The insurance policy was therefore not valid, and Sarah received no compensation for the loss of her car.

cars and motorcycles

AT WHAT AGE?

At 14 you can ride an electrically powered pedal cycle.

At 16 you can ride a moped up to 50cc, a small tractor or a mowing machine. If you receive a disability living allowance at the higher rate you can also drive an invalid carriage or a car.

At 17 you can drive a car with up to eight passenger seats, a motor tricycle, an invalid carriage, a motorbike up to 125cc, a large tractor and a van or lorry up to 3.5 tons.

At 18 you can drive a van or lorry up to 7.5 tons.

At 21 you can drive all other vehicles. For hiring a car, most car hire companies have a minimum age of between 21 and 23.

Traffic offences

Every vehicle on the road must meet a whole set of regulations covering brakes, tyres, lights, mirrors, steering and even windscreen washer bottles (which must, by law, never be empty).

A police officer may stop a vehicle at any time to check that it is in roadworthy condition, and it is no excuse for the driver to claim that they didn't realise a light wasn't working. These are absolute offences and apply even if the driver was completely unaware of the problem.

If the police believe a vehicle is not roadworthy they can instruct the driver to get it checked and repaired by a garage (usually within 14 days), give the driver a fixed penalty, or call up a specially trained vehicle examiner to inspect the car or bike there and then. A police officer who feels a vehicle is so dangerous that someone will probably be injured if it is used any further, can immediately ban it from being driven.

Cycling

Cyclists are expected to follow the same basic laws as other road users. They have a duty of care to pedestrians, other riders and road users. It is an offence, under the *Roads (Scotland) Act 1984* to ride a bicycle (or tricycle) on the pavement. Careless or dangerous cycling are also offences under road traffic law.

There is no breath test for cyclists; a court would instead be guided by evidence from the officer who made the arrest. Enforcement of cycling offences is up to the local police.

BUYING A CAR

- A small popular car is usually less of a risk. Spare parts are cheaper and easier to obtain, insurance costs lower and it will probably be easier to sell when you want to change it.
- A car bought privately is usually cheaper than one bought from a dealer, but you have fewer rights if things go wrong. The Sale of Goods Act 1979 (see money, page 52), gives greater protection if you buy from a dealer. A car bought privately need only be "as described". The legal expression "caveat emptor" (meaning "buyer beware"), particularly applies when buying a second-hand car. It is notoriously difficult to get problems sorted out once you have paid for the car.
- Look at the car in daylight. Take someone along with you who knows about cars. Check the owner's purchase documents to see if any hire-purchase payments are still due. The RAC, AA or Green Flag will inspect and report on the mechanical state of the car, check on the HP payments and tell you whether the car has been stolen or is an insurance write-off. HPI Autodata or AA Car Data provide a similar service at a slightly lower cost, without the mechanical inspection.
- Look to see if the car's mileage tallies with the MOT certificate and the service history. You can also check with previous owners. Ask the dealer if they have tried to verify the mileage - they have to do this by law. Be wary if there is a sticker on the speedometer indicating that there is no guarantee that the mileage is accurate.
- Ask to see the Vehicle Registration Certificate (V5C). If it's a private sale, it should contain the seller's name and address. It also gives the Vehicle Identification Number (VIN), which should correspond with the number stamped on identification plates under the bonnet and on the floor. If you have any doubts, leave the car alone.
- If you buy a car that turns out to be stolen, it remains the property of the true owner - meaning that you will almost certainly lose your money, unless you can get it back from the person from whom you bought the car.

■ BRIEF CASE: Anna

Anna went to look at a Ford Escort, advertised privately in her local paper. She asked the seller if the car had been in an accident. He said no, but having bought the car, Anna later found evidence of major crash repairs. She went back to the seller, pointed out the car was not as described and eventually got her money back.

However, if the car had just been unreliable (even breaking down on her first drive), there is probably little she could have done, as there is nothing in law that states that a car bought privately must be of satisfactory or reasonable quality.

driving

Safety

Seat belts and crash helmets

Seat belts (front and rear), where fitted, must be worn by drivers and passengers. If a passenger in your car does not wear a belt, it is he or she who will be prosecuted, not you - unless the passenger is under 14, when it is your responsibility. Children under 12 and under four feet five inches (1.35m) tall must use the appropriate child restraint - seat, booster seat, or cushion - for their weight.

Motorcyclist and pillion passengers must both wear an approved safety helmet on all journeys. This regulation does not apply to a follower of the Sikh religion while he is wearing a turban. Tinted visors may only be used if they let enough light through, otherwise they are illegal.

SPEED LIMITS

Cars and motorcycles are limited to
- **30 mph in built-up areas,**
- **60 mph on single carriageways,**
- **70 mph on dual carriageways and motorways.**

Speed limits for buses, lorries, and cars towing caravans are lower.
The presence of street lights generally means a 30mph speed limit unless otherwise indicated.

Speeding

Speeding is an absolute offence, which means that it is no defence to say that it wasn't dangerous or that you didn't realise that you were breaking the speed limit. Offenders usually receive a fixed fine and penalty points.

If you break the speed limit, or are seen by the police to be driving carelessly or dangerously, you must be warned of the possibility of prosecution at the time of the offence or served with a summons within 14 days of the offence; otherwise you cannot be convicted, unless an accident occurred at the time or immediately after.

Driving badly

Careless driving is to drive in a way that is not how a careful and reasonable driver would behave. Pulling out from a side road without looking is an example of this. Dangerous driving is to drive in a way that is dangerous to people or property, such as driving very fast through a built-up area or overtaking on a sharp bend. Dangerous driving and causing death by dangerous driving are very serious offences, which courts will punish with fines, disqualification, and imprisonment. If you face such a charge, get in touch with a solicitor straightaway.

Stolen vehicles

Stealing a vehicle to sell on to someone else is theft. Joyriding, or taking a car to ride around in and then dumping it, is a different offence, under the *Road Traffic Act 1988*.

Mobile phones

It is an offence for drivers to use a hand held mobile phone while driving; this includes waiting at traffic lights or in a traffic jam – except to call 999 or 112 in a genuine emergency. Motorists may be given a fixed penalty of £60.00 and collect three penalty points, with fines rising to £1,000 if convicted in court and £2,500 for drivers of vans, buses and lorries.

use the law with care try talking first

■ **BRIEF CASE: Peter**

Peter was involved in a crash with a motorcycle. He feared that it was his fault and that he would lose his licence, as he already had a number of penalty points. He persuaded his wife Sophie, who was not in the car at the time, to tell the police that it was she who was driving. A week later they both admitted the deception, but were charged with perverting the course of justice. Peter and Sophie were sentenced to four and two months in prison.

brief case

anyone whom they reasonably suspect of driving with excess alcohol, who is involved in a traffic offence or road accident, however minor, even if there is no suspicion of alcohol. A uniformed police officer is also entitled to stop motorists at random in order to see whether there is a reasonable suspicion that they have consumed any alcohol. If there is, the officer can go on to ask the motorist to take a breath test.

If the test is positive or the driver refuses a breath test, the driver will be arrested and taken to a police station for further tests.

No escape A driver who fails to blow into the device properly, or refuses to take a test, will still end up with a heavy fine and have his or her licence endorsed with three to eleven penalty points. Courts rarely accept that there are special reasons for drivers being over the limit. Disqualification from driving is almost automatic. A drunken driver who causes someone's death may be sent to prison for up to 14 years, will be disqualified from driving for at least two years, and given obligatory penalty points on their licence.

Drinking and driving

Alcohol seriously affects a driver's judgement and reactions. There is no law that limits a driver to a certain number of drinks, such as two pints of beer or one glass of wine, but there is a maximum amount of alcohol that you may have in your body while driving or being in charge of a car. In law, being in charge of a car might include simply sitting in the seat of a parked car, though each case will depend on its own circumstances.

The limits Currently, a driver will be found guilty of drink-driving if he or she has more than 80mg alcohol in 100ml of blood. However, in 2013, the Scottish Government announced its intention to reduce this limit to 50mg alcohol in 100ml of blood – a figure that would bring Scotland into line with much of the rest of Europe.

Breath tests The police will carry out a road side breath test to check whether a driver has more than the permitted amount of alcohol in their body. Uniformed police can breathalyse

■ **BRIEF CASE: Jean**

Jean had had too much to drink at a party, she didn't want to stay at the house and decided to sleep it off on the back seat of her car. She was woken by the police, breathalysed and found to be over the limit. Although she said she had no intention of driving she was successfully prosecuted and lost her licence for 18 months.

brief case

driving

Penalty points Most motoring offences are dealt with through a system of penalty points that are entered on a driver's licence. Anyone receiving twelve or more points within a period of three years will almost always be disqualified from driving for at least six months. Details of the points carried for each offence are given in the Highway Code. Drivers, who have six or more penalty points on their licence within two years of their test, go back to being a learner until they pass a further test.

accidents

What to do Accidents happen to the most careful of drivers, often through no fault of their own. If you are involved in an accident, there are certain things that you should and should not do...

- Stop immediately. Try to stay calm, even if people are yelling and screaming at you.
- Check that everyone involved is OK. If anyone is injured, call an ambulance before you do anything else.
- You must give your name and address and details of your vehicle to anyone who has reasonable need to know them. This includes a police officer at the scene of the accident, anyone who is injured, anyone whose property is damaged and the owner of any animal injured or killed. (This applies to horses, cows, sheep, goats and dogs - but not cats.) If someone is injured, you must also produce your insurance certificate to show that you are properly insured. If you can't do this at the time of the accident, then you must give this information to the police as soon as possible and certainly within 24 hours. If you don't, you will be committing an offence.
- Make sure you get the name, address, vehicle registration number and insurance details of the other drivers involved.
- Contact your insurance company as soon as possible, and also make a detailed note of everything that happened. This should cover the time of day, weather, light, estimated speeds, position of vehicles before and after the accident, what people said and anything else that you think might be relevant. If you can, take photos before anything is moved, or draw a sketch plan as soon as you feel able to do so.
- Don't drive away without stopping. It is a criminal offence.
- Be cautious if the other driver suggests not calling the police and offers you cash to cover the damage. It might be an offence not to report the accident, and you may find that the damage to your vehicle costs a lot more than you are being offered. If someone is injured in the accident it is an offence not to report it to the police.
- Don't admit it was your fault. You may find later that the other driver was drunk, driving too fast, or without lights - in which case you might not be to blame at all. If you do admit responsibility, your words may end up by being used against you in court and may affect your insurance claim.

INDIVIDUALS
ENGAGING IN
SOCIETY

Citizenship Foundation

powers & duties

Powers and duties

Most of the information that the police receive comes from the general public. Without this help they could do very little.

Much of the law dealing with police powers and duties when investigating crime, along with the rights of those who have been arrested or are being questioned, is contained in the *Criminal Procedure (Scotland) Act 1995*.

The Act sets out rules that the police must follow when searching for and collecting evidence. If the rules are broken, a judge or sheriff may decide that the evidence obtained cannot be used in court, and the police officers concerned may be disciplined.

POLICE DISCIPLINE

Police officers must obey both the law of the land, and their own code of discipline. This discipline code is broken if an officer:
- unreasonably neglects their duty,
- makes a false written or spoken statement,
- misuses their authority, eg through unnecessary violence,
- is rude or abusive,
- behaves in a discriminatory way, relating to gender, race, religion, or sexual orientation.

The Police have a legal duty to promote racial equality and good relations between people of different racial groups.

stop & search

Stop!

If a police officer stops you in the street, you are entitled to know the officer's name and the police station at which they are based. You are also entitled to know why the officer has stopped you. It is not acceptable for this to be simply because of your colour, dress, hairstyle, or the fact that you might have been in trouble before.

Strictly speaking, you don't have to answer a police officer's questions, but someone who refuses to give their name and address may well find themselves detained or arrested if the officer believes that they have something to hide.

If a police officer has reasonable grounds to suspect that you have committed or are committing an offence, the officer can require you to give your name, address, date and place of birth, along with your nationality. However, reasonable suspicion is a subjective term and will vary from one situation to another. So, before you can be required to give this information, the officer must first describe the basis for their suspicion.

A police officer is entitled to use reasonable force to ensure that you do not run away whilst the information is checked. You have the right not to answer any more questions until you have received legal advice, see page 115.

Stay calm

If you're stopped by the police, keep calm and don't overreact. If you're obstructive and rude, you're more likely to be arrested and you may also be charged with resisting them in the execution of their duty.

use the law with care try talking first

Staying calm will also help you remember what happened and what was said. If you deliberately mislead the police by giving false information or wasting their time, you risk a fine or even imprisonment.

Search!

People

The police do not have the power to search anyone they choose, but they can search someone (and the vehicle in which they are travelling), who has been arrested or is suspected of carrying:

- **illegal drugs,**
- **stolen property,**
- **an offensive weapon,**
- **alcohol, if you are at or travelling on public transport to a major football or rugby match,**
- **fireworks unlawfully, or**
- **anything that might be used for the hunting or poaching of animals.**

Any search involving more than a check of your outer clothing should be done out of public view or in a police station or van. If the search requires more than the removal of outer clothing, it should be done by someone of the same sex.

An intimate search, for example looking for drugs hidden inside a person's body, may be conducted only by a warrant from a sheriff.

In the know

If you, or the vehicle in which you are travelling, are searched by the police, the officer should state beforehand why the search is taking place and what they expect to find. You have every right to ask for an explanation if this has not been made clear.

If the police search you illegally, a judge or sheriff may decide that the evidence obtained cannot be used in court. The police will normally make a written record of the outcome of their search, particularly if they find something illegal, like controlled drugs or an offensive weapon.

stop & search

Property The police do not have the power to enter and search any house or building that they choose. But they are allowed to carry out a search if:

- **they have the agreement of the occupier of the building, or**
- **they have a warrant (or permission) from a court, or**
- **it is necessary due to urgency, eg, in order to catch an escaped prisoner, save life, prevent serious property damage, or to prevent certain kinds of disturbance.**

If possible, the police should explain why they are making the search and should keep a record of whether they needed to use force to get in, any damage caused, and anything they took away.

Special powers Police powers of search are extended in certain circumstances by the *Criminal Justice and Public Order Act 1994*. If a senior police officer believes that a serious violent incident might take place in the area, or that dangerous weapons are being carried, he or she can give officers the authority to stop any person or vehicle to search for the weapons. This applies even when the constable has no grounds for suspecting that the person stopped might have broken the law.

detention and arrest

Under the *Criminal Procedure (Scotland) Act 1995* there are two types of situation, namely detention and arrest, where the police can take a person under the care and control of the law. This means that for the time being, the suspect loses certain freedoms - such as to go and do as they please - but, in return, has certain rights designed to protect them from unreasonable treatment.

Detention If the police do not have enough evidence to bring a charge, they may take the suspect into legal custody to carry out further investigations.

If you are detained in this way, the police must have reasonable grounds for suspecting you have committed an offence which is punishable by imprisonment. The police must take you as quickly as possible to a police station and inform you of their suspicion, of the general nature of the alleged offence, and the reason for the detention

In most circumstances, you may be detained for a maximum of 12 hours, by the end of

HELPING THE POLICE WITH THEIR ENQUIRIES

If you are asked to go to a police station to help with enquiries, it's important to know if you are being arrested, or whether the decision to attend is up to you. If you are being asked to go voluntarily, you may refuse - although the police may then decide to detain or arrest you - and then you have to go. If you go to the police station voluntarily, you may leave at any time you wish, unless during that time the police detain or arrest you.

You are entitled to send a message to your family or a friend telling them where you are, and to receive free legal advice from a solicitor, even though you are attending the police station voluntarily.

which time the police must arrest you, detain you on other grounds, or release you without charge. In very serious cases, detention may be extended to 24 hours.

If you are detained, you do not need to answer any questions but you must provide your name, address, date of birth, place of birth, and nationality.

You are entitled to have someone, such as a parent or solicitor, told without delay of your whereabouts and circumstances. (If you are under 16, the police must contact your parents or guardian.) However, as a detained person you don't have the right to see a solicitor before or during the police interview.

Arrest Arrest is a more serious form of legal custody than detention, and a charge should follow on from arrest without undue delay. If you are arrested, you are entitled to:

- **know the reason for your arrest,**
- **have a solicitor informed of where you are,**
- **know whether you will be released or taken to court (and, if so, where), and**
- **a private interview with your solicitor before your first appearance in court**

You should be told about these rights and cautioned – see page 116.

at the police station

Legal advice & the caution

If the police believe that you have committed an offence and want to question you further, they must first caution you by saying: *"You are going to be asked questions about (description of crime). You are not bound to answer but, if you do your answers will be noted and may be used in evidence"*. This means that if the case goes to court, any answers you initially gave may be used in court as evidence against you. However, the fact that you exercised your legal right to remain silent cannot be used against you.

If you have been arrested or have been detained and are being questioned, it is better not to answer questions (except your name, address, date of birth, place of birth and nationality) until you have had a chance to speak to a solicitor – see page 115.

Vulnerable people

Anyone detained or arrested by the police who is in vulnerable state (through perhaps mental illness or a learning disability) should not normally be interviewed without an "appropriate adult" present. This is someone who is entirely independent and able to help the person understand what is going on, and make sure that they are being properly treated.

Interviews

There are clear rules governing the way police officers can question a person, which are designed to stop unfair pressure being placed on a suspect.

There should be regular breaks for food, and the cell and interview room should be clean, properly heated, ventilated, and lit. Someone who is deaf or has difficulty in understanding English should be given a signer or an interpreter.

Your interview at the police station may be recorded on tape or CD. If the interview is not recorded, the police officers interviewing you will make notes of the interview in their police notebook. At the end of the interview, they will normally ask you to sign these notes to confirm that you agree that they are a fair record of what was said.

Fingerprints and photographs

If you have been detained or arrested, the police can take fingerprints and DNA samples (such as hair cuttings or mouth swabs) - and you must allow them to do so. However, the police are not allowed to conduct an internal physical examination unless the Procurator Fiscal has first obtained a warrant from a sheriff.

Fingerprints, DNA samples and photographs must be destroyed if the person is charged, and found not guilty, or not charged at all.

Release or custody

After arresting you, the police must decide what to do next. If there is enough evidence, they can:

- **release you and report the circumstances to the Procurator Fiscal or Children's Reporter who will decide on further action;**
- **release you on a written signed undertaking (also known as a bail-undertaking) requiring you to appear at a named court on a named date; or**
- **keep you in custody to appear in court; this must be on the next day, not including weekends, bank holidays or court holidays.**

Bail If you appear in court from custody, the court must consider the issue of bail on your first appearance. The law states that you should normally be released on bail, unless there is good reason to refuse: if, for example, there is a risk that you would run away or not turn up again in court, or that you might interfere with witnesses.

If you are granted bail there are standard conditions which must be followed: that you appear at a named court, on a named date, and that you be of "good behaviour".

The court may also attach special conditions; for example, you may be required to report to the police station once a week, to take part in an ID parade, or to avoid a particular location.

If the court refuses bail, it must give the reasons for this decision.

A person with previous convictions for violent or sexual offences or repeated drug trafficking will only be given bail if the court considers that there are exceptional circumstances that justify doing so.

orders, contracts and notices

Anti-social behaviour notices

A court order prohibiting someone from committing specific anti-social acts, or from entering a certain area. ASBOs are designed to stop behaviour that causes people distress or alarm, and can be used with anyone aged 12 or over.

Acceptable behaviour contracts

This is an agreement between the young person, their parent or carer and a local agency such as the police or a housing authority, listing the kinds of anti-social behaviour that the young person promises not to get involved with, along with other measures that they (or their parent or carer) agree to undertake.

Fixed penalty notices

Police officers and certain other authorised officers have the power to issue a fine, known as a fixed penalty notice, to anyone committing certain offences, such as dropping litter or smoking in no-smoking premises. If the fine is paid within the required period, the person does not receive a criminal record. If it is not paid, details will be forwarded to the Procurator Fiscal who may choose to issue another fine or to prepare the case for trial.

COMPLAINTS AGAINST THE POLICE

If you feel that you have suffered, or witnessed police misconduct, you may decide that you want to make an official complaint.

Think about what happened; make sure you are clear what was wrong. If it is a serious matter, it's a good idea to speak to a solicitor, local councillor, or MSP beforehand. A 'complaints against the police' leaflet should be available at your local police office and will provide information on how the complaint should be made and how it will be investigated.

You can make your complaint by telephone, letter, email, or in person at a police station. You can also ask a solicitor, MSP, or local councillor to take up the matter on your behalf.

In reply, you may get an apology, or an explanation of the officer's conduct. If you are still not satisfied you can refer the matter to the Police Investigations and Review Commissioner, see contacts.

use the law with care try talking first

Most terrorist offences are already against the law, but the police now have extra powers to help them with their enquiries.

Definition

Terrorism refers to actions designed to advance a political, religious or ideological cause, which deliberately...

- **cause serious violence or damage,**
- **threaten or intimidate members of the public,**
- **create a public health or safety risk, or**
- **interfere with electronic communications.**

Police powers

The police can use stop and search powers to see if someone is a terrorist even if they do not have any grounds for suspecting the person of committing an offence.

They can specify areas where, for up to 28 days, people and vehicles may be randomly stopped and searched without evidence of illegal activity.

Premises can often be searched without a warrant and a senior police officer can authorise emergency searches if it is believed to be "in the interests of the state".

Areas can be cordoned off to allow the police to search for evidence of terrorism.

Detention

Terrorist suspects can be detained by the police without charge for up to 14 days (and this may be extended to 28 days). Access to a solicitor can be delayed for 48 hours.

Under the *Protection of Terrorism Act 2005*, the government can place people

they suspect of terrorism under house arrest, even though they don't have enough evidence to go to court to prove an offence.

Other powers

Some organisations are forbidden - known as "proscribed" - which means that it is illegal to be a member of them. The list contains suspected terrorist organisations from around the world.

Since the bomb attacks in London in July 2005, the police have been given extra powers under the *Terrorism Act 2006*. It is now an offence to prepare a terrorist act, to give or receive terrorist training, and to sell or distribute terrorist publications.

"Praising or celebrating" terrorism in a way which could encourage others to carry out a terrorist act can lead to a being arrested and charged with the "glorification of terrorism".

courts

The job of investigating a crime and charging a suspect is done by the police, but the decision as to whether to continue with the case and bring it to court is made by the Crown Office Procurator Fiscal Service (COPFS).

Fiscals are legal qualified civil servants, independent from the police, who decide, on the basis of the information supplied by the police, whether there is sufficient evidence that a crime has been committed and, if so, what action should be taken. The COPFS may decide not to take any further action, to prosecute, or to deal with the case in some other way, perhaps through a warning letter or fine.

Summary or solemn?
Crimes in Scotland can be prosecuted at two levels: *summary* or *solemn*.

Prosecution at summary level involves less serious crimes and covers trials in the Justice of the Peace Court and the Sheriff Court.

If you are to be prosecuted at summary level, you or your solicitor will receive a Copy Complaint. This is usually served through the post by COPFS and tells you the nature of the charge. It usually also includes a summary of evidence and a list of any previous convictions. It will also tell you at what court you must appear and at what level you will be prosecuted. A letter will also be enclosed telling you the date and time of your first appearance in court.

Prosecution at solemn level deals with more serious crimes. This covers trials in the Sheriff Court and the High Court. If you are to be prosecuted at solemn level, you or your solicitor will receive a petition. The petition tells you the nature of the charge and includes a summary of evidence, but does not include a list of your previous convictions.

Age of criminal responsibility
In Scotland, children are considered responsible for their criminal actions from the age of eight, but no child under 12 may be prosecuted.

Children's panel court
If you are aged between 12 and 15 and commit a criminal offence, your case will probably be referred to a children's panel. Cases involving people aged 16 or 17 are dealt with in the children's panel system or by a court. Cases involving those aged 18 or over are handled within the adult court system.

use the law with care try talking first

Justice of the peace court

This court hears only summary criminal cases, ie cases of a less serious nature. Justices are not legally qualified, but are members of standing in the local community. In court, they are advised on the law by a qualified lawyer, called their legal assessor. Cases are usually heard by one justice, but in some areas, three justices sit as a panel.

In the justice of the peace court Glasgow, cases are also heard by a stipendiary magistrate. Stipendiary magistrates are legally qualified and only ever sit alone. They have greater sentencing powers than a justice of the peace.

Sheriff Court

The Sheriff Court deals with criminal cases at both summary and solemn level; however the most serious cases are heard in the High Court of Justiciary.

Cases in the Sheriff Court are heard by a sheriff, a qualified lawyer with at least ten years' experience. The sheriff sits alone in summary cases and with a jury in solemn cases.

High Court of Justiciary

The High Court of Justiciary deals only with the most serious offences such as murder, serious assault and armed robbery. The High Court sits permanently in Edinburgh and Glasgow but can also travel around the country as required.

courts

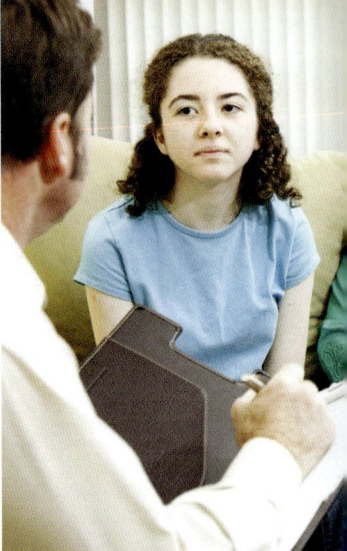

Legal Aid and advice

Legal aid allows people to get financial help with the cost of their legal advice and representation in court. Generally, applications are made by a solicitor to the Scottish Legal Aid Board.

If you are charged with an offence, it is important to get legal advice as soon as possible. If you have a solicitor, you can ask for them to be notified of your situation. If you don't have a solicitor, ask for the duty solicitor. It is the duty solicitor's job to represents people who don't have their own solicitor.

You can find a solicitor by phoning the Scottish Legal Aid Board or searching online, see **contacts**.

Juries

The job of a jury is to decide whether or not, on the facts of a criminal case, the accused is guilty or not guilty. The charge against an accused person can also be found not proven, in which case the accused is acquitted. A jury can convict on a majority of 8-7.

A jury is made up of 15 adults (not 12, as in England and Wales), aged between 18-70, who have lived in Britain for a continuous period of at least five years from the age of 13. They are chosen at random from the local electoral register (see page 130), but there are certain categories of people who cannot be selected. These include judges, magistrates, ministers of religion, prison, police and probation officers, anyone on bail or who has been on probation within the last five years, and anyone sentenced to prison, detention centre, youth custody or community service within the last ten years.

If you are called as a member of a jury, you will usually be given about six weeks' notice. Although some people, such as MPs, members of the armed forces and the medical profession have the right to be excused, it is normally compulsory. But if there is a strong reason why you are unable to serve, you may be excused or allowed to defer your service. Contact the sheriff clerk at the court as soon as possible. Jurors are able to claim the cost of travel to court and a small financial allowance.

Going to court

See **contacts** for details about going to court as a witness or juror.

law
government
and human rights

INDIVIDUALS
ENGAGING IN
SOCIETY

Citizenship Foundation

making the law

The Scottish Parliament

The Scottish Parliament began sitting in 1999. It was set up by the *Scotland Act 1998* following a Scotland-wide referendum in 1997. It is made up of Members of the Scottish Parliament (MSPs). A First Minister is elected by the MSPs and he or she, together with a team of Ministers, forms the Scottish Government. The Scottish Parliament is able to make laws for Scotland on any subject, except for certain matters which are reserved to the United Kingdom Parliament. One such reserved matter is taxation; however the Scottish Parliament does have the power to vary to some extent the rate of income tax which applies to Scottish taxpayers.

A law made by the Scottish Parliament begins its life as a Bill. Bills are put forward by the Scottish Government, by individual MSPs, or by one of the Scottish Parliament's committees. If the Scottish Parliament votes in favour of the Bill, it will be given the Royal Assent, and is known as an Act of the Scottish Parliament.

SCOTTISH INDEPENDENCE

In March 2013, Alex Salmond, the First Minister of Scotland, announced that a referendum will be held on the 18th September 2014 on whether Scotland should leave the United Kingdom and become an independent sovereign state.

The UK Parliament

The United Kingdom Parliament sits in Westminster, in London. Only the UK Parliament can pass laws on certain matters, such as the economy, foreign policy, social security, energy, employment, broadcasting, and some medical issues. (These are known as reserved matters, on which the Scottish Parliament cannot act.)

In theory, the UK Parliament could still pass laws relating to other Scottish issues but, in practice, it would only do so with the agreement of the Scottish Parliament.

The United Kingdom Parliament is made up of two bodies: the House of Commons and the House of Lords. The Commons comprises elected Members of Parliament (MPs), and the Lords is made up of unelected peers.

Bills can be proposed either by the Government (led by the Prime Minister), or by an individual MP or peer. The latter are known as *private members' Bills*. To become law, a Bill must be passed by the House of Commons, and receive the Royal Assent, and is then known as an Act of Parliament. As a general rule, the House of Lords can only delay, but not prevent, a Bill from becoming an Act of Parliament. Nor can the Queen refuse to give the Royal Assent.

The Scottish legal system

Scotland has a separate and different legal system from England and Wales, in which Scots law is applied.

Scots law is made up of laws passed by the Scottish Parliament, the UK Parliament, and the old Scottish Parliament (which existed before Scotland united with England in 1707), as well as certain legal texts written by Scottish lawyers in the 17th and 18th centuries, and the decisions of other judges in previous cases.

Judges do not make new laws, but their decisions may develop the law. A specially convened court with a large number of judges can overrule old cases; recently a special court of seven judges changed the way that rape is defined in Scotland.

European law

Since the United Kingdom joined the European Community (now the European Union) in 1973, European law has become increasingly important in Scotland. European law is made by the European Parliament, the European Commission and the Council of the European Union. It covers a wide variety of areas, such as agriculture and employment rights. Sometimes the UK and Scottish Parliaments have to pass laws to bring the countries in line with European law. However, certain types of European law can be used in Scottish courts without the Scottish or UK Governments having to take any action.

It is unlawful for the Scottish Parliament to pass any legislation that is incompatible with European law; if it did do this, the law could be challenged in a Scottish court.

■ BRIEF CASE

brief case

One day in August 1928, 30-year-old May Donoghue met a friend at the Wellmeadow Café in Paisley, where May's friend ordered pears and ice-cream for herself and ginger beer and ice-cream for May. When the ginger beer was brought to their table, it was in a dark bottle, and was poured over the ice cream. May took a drink, and then tipped the rest of the bottle into her glass, and was shocked to see the remains of a snail.

The thought of what she had just drunk made May feel very ill. With bad stomach pains and gastro-enteritis, she went to her doctor, and later to the Glasgow Royal Infirmary.

As a result of what had happened, May decided to sue the manufacturer of the ginger beer. As she had no contract with the manufacturer, it was argued that she had no right to damages. However, this was believed to be an important case, and it was eventually heard by the Law Lords who decided that the manufacturer had a legal duty of care to anyone who consumed its product.

This case became the foundation of our law of negligence, which allows us, in certain circumstances, to claim money from those who carelessly cause injury or damage.

Similarly, the Scottish Government cannot act in breach of European law.

human rights

European Convention on Human Rights

This is an international agreement, drawn up by the Council of Europe to protect people's human rights after the horrors of the Second World War. It took effect in 1953 and sets out fundamental rights and freedoms that everybody should have, along with the limited circumstances in which they may be restricted by the state.

Forty seven states, including the UK, have signed the Convention, and all are expected to uphold it terms. If anyone believes that the UK has breached the Convention, they may take their case to the European Court of Human Rights in Strasbourg. However, as a result of the *Scotland Act 1998*, the rights of the Convention are directly enforceable in Scottish courts.

The Scotland Act 1998

Under the *Scotland Act*, the Scottish Parliament cannot pass any laws that are incompatible with the European Convention on Human Rights. Nor can the Scottish Government (which includes the Lord Advocate, who is head of the criminal prosecution system in Scotland) take action that is incompatible with the Convention.

■ BRIEF CASE: A CHANGE IN THE LAW

In September 1976, Jeffrey Cosans, aged 16, took a short cut home from school in Cowdenbeath through a nearby cemetery. This was against school rules and Jeffrey was reported to the head, who decided that the boy should be punished with the strap. Jeffrey refused, and was supported by his parents, who said that they thought corporal punishment was morally wrong. Jeffrey was suspended.

Both the school and the local authority suggested various ways in which he might be allowed back – but could not promise that Jeffrey would not be beaten again for misbehaviour. Jeffrey's parents would not agree to this. They claimed that the local authority were breaking part of the European Convention on Human Rights, which says that no one shall be denied the right to education and that parents have the right to make sure that their children are taught in a way that respects their religious and philosophical beliefs.

When the case eventually reached the European Court of Human Rights in 1982, the Court agreed with Jeffrey's mother, who had made the application. As a result, the British government had to change the law on corporal punishment in schools. This took some time to achieve, but corporal punishment was eventually abolished in most UK schools in 1987, and is now banned in all UK schools.

use the law with care **try talking first**

torture and killing, extending to people's rights in everyday life: what they can say and do, their beliefs, their right to a fair trial and many other similar basic entitlements.

(Article 1 is introductory)

Human Rights Act 1998

The *Human Rights Act* came into force in October 2000, incorporating most of the human rights set out in the European Convention into the law of Scotland and the rest of the UK.

Under the Act, all laws must, as far as possible, be compatible with the rights listed in the Convention, and public bodies – such as the armed forces, local authorities, schools, hospitals, the police, prisons and the courts – must carry out their work in a way that respects these basic human rights. If they don't, then the law or the actions of the public body can be challenged in our own courts.

If the courts decide that a law is incompatible with the rights in the Convention, it is for the UK Government and Parliament to decide how to proceed, and whether to amend the legislation.

Using the Act

If you believe that a public body has broken your rights under the Convention, you can challenge this by bringing an action against the body concerned. You can also rely on a Convention right in your defence if a public authority brings an action against you.

The Convention Rights in UK law

There are 16 fundamental rights in the Act. They go beyond matters of life and death, like freedom from

Article 2 Right to life

Everyone has the absolute right to have their life protected by law. There are only certain very limited circumstances where it is acceptable for the state to take away someone's life, eg if a police officer acts justifiably in self-defence. The Human Rights Act completely abolished the death penalty in the UK.

Article 3 Prohibition of torture

Everyone has the absolute right not to be tortured or subjected to treatment or punishment that is inhuman or degrading. The UK cannot deport someone to a country where they are likely to suffer torture or face the death penalty.

Article 4 Prohibition of slavery and forced labour

Everyone has the absolute right not to be treated as a slave or forced to perform forced or compulsory labour.

Article 5 Right to liberty and security

Everyone has the right not to be deprived of their liberty – 'arrested or detained' – except in limited cases specified in the Article (eg where they are suspected of convicted of committing a crime) and where this is justified by a clear legal procedure.

human rights

Article 6 Right to a fair trial

Everyone has the right to a fair and public hearing within a reasonable period of time. This applies to both civil and criminal proceedings. Hearings must be by an independent and impartial tribunal established by law. It is possible to exclude the public from the hearing (though not the judgment) in order to protect national security or public order. Anyone facing a criminal charge is presumed innocent until proved guilty according to law and has certain minimum guaranteed rights to defend themselves.

Article 7 No punishment without law

Everyone has the right to be protected from being found guilty of an offence if it wasn't against the law at the time it was committed. There is also protection against changes in the law which increase the possible sentence or the type of punishment for an offence.

Articles 8–11

The rights to freedoms in Articles 8-11 may be restricted where it is necessary to protect things like public health or safety, the rights of others, or to prevent crime. Interference with these rights that goes too far can be challenged in the courts who will try to strike a fair balance.

Article 8 Right to respect for private life

Everyone has the right to respect for their private and family life, their home and their correspondence.

Article 9 Freedom of conscience, thought and religion

Everyone is free to hold whatever views, beliefs and thoughts (including religious faith) they like.

Article 10 Freedom of expression

Everyone has the right to express their views on their own or in a group. This applies even if they are unpopular or disturbing. This right can be restricted in specified circumstances.

Article 11 Freedom of assembly and association

Everyone has the right to get together with other people in a peaceful way. They also have the right to associate with other people, which includes the right to form a trade union. These rights may be restricted only in specified circumstances.

Article 12 Right to marry

Men and women have the right to marry and start a family (a right that is likely to be extended to same-sex couples in 2014). Our national law still governs how and at what age this can take place.

(Article 13, which deals with legal remedies, is not incorporated into our law)

Article 14 Prohibition of discrimination

Everyone has the right to benefit from these Convention rights regardless of race, religion, sex, political views or any other status, unless a restriction can be reasonably justified.

HOW DOES THE HUMAN RIGHTS ACT AFFECT US?

The *Human Rights Act* is a unique type of higher law, affecting all other laws. The rights and their limitations are a set of basic values. Respect for these rights and everything that goes with them may help change the way people think and behave. It is designed to create a society in which decisions and policies are better discussed and understood. But the freedoms protected by the Act are not a complete set of human values and do not, for example, include the right to work or freedom from poverty.

The Act cannot be used directly by one private individual against another. It is designed to indicate how judges in courts must interpret the law and how public bodies – such as the police, the prison service and local councils – must carry out their actions.

It protects fundamental freedoms – like liberty and free speech – but also allows limits to be placed on these rights in order to try to make sure that other people are also treated fairly.

For example, a person's right to liberty may be restricted if they are guilty of a serious crime. This is for other people's protection. Similarly there are limits placed on freedom of speech to prevent someone from expressing views that are likely to incite hatred or endanger national security.

Article 1 of Protocol 1*
Protection of property

Everyone has the right to the peaceful enjoyment of their possessions. Public authorities cannot usually interfere with things we own or the way we use them, except in specified limited circumstances.

Article 2 of Protocol 1*
Right to education

Everyone has the right to access to an effective education.

Article 3 of Protocol 1*
Right to free elections

Elections must be free and fair, and take place by secret ballot. Some restrictions can be placed on those who are allowed to vote, eg by setting a minimum age.

Articles 1 and 2 of Protocol 6*
Abolition of the death penalty

These provisions abolish the death penalty.

* a 'protocol' is a later addition to the Convention)

voting & elections

Who can vote?

You are generally entitled to vote in the various Scottish elections if you are aged 18 or over on the day of an election, and your name is on the electoral register maintained by your local council.

To vote in a local election and elections to the Scottish and European Parliaments, you must live in the local area and be a citizen of the UK, the European Union, or the Commonwealth.

For UK Parliamentary elections, voters must be UK, Irish, or Commonwealth citizens, and either live in the UK or, if abroad, be registered in the UK as an overseas voter.

Who can't vote?

Those people who can't vote in Scotland include anyone not on the electoral register, most people compulsorily held for treatment for mental illness, anyone convicted of corrupt practices at an election during the previous five years, and members of the House of Lords.

Registering to vote

The electoral register is a list of names and addresses of everyone who is eligible to vote; you can't vote in an election if your name is not on the register.

Each year, between July and November, local councils deliver electoral registration forms to every home in Scotland. Householders are required by law to complete and return the form, with the name of everyone in that household aged 16 or over – although you are not eligible to vote until you are 18.

If you are a student, you can register to vote at both your home and term-time addresses.

A new electoral register (also known as the electoral roll) is published on 1st December each year. You can check if your name is on the register at your local electoral registration office.

However, you can also register to vote at any time by contacting your local council election registration office or downloading a form from *www.aboutmyvote.co.uk*

SCOTTISH INDEPENDENCE

At the end of June 2013, MSPs approved the Scottish Referendum (Franchise) Bill giving 16 and 17-year-olds the right to vote in the forthcoming referendum for independence (although not the right to vote in other elections).

Those entitled to vote will be people who were born on or before 18th September 1998, who live in Scotland and are registered to vote, and are citizens of Britain, Ireland, or other EU countries, or of the Commonwealth, or members of the armed services serving overseas.

use the law with care try talking first

LOCAL COUNCILLOR, MSP, MP OR MEP?

You can stand for political office from the age of 18. If you want to be a local councillor you must either:

- **be registered to vote in the local authority area;**
- **have lived in the local authority area during the whole of the last 12 months;**
- **had your main or only place of work in the local authority area during the whole of the last 12 months; or**
- **have occupied any land or premises in the local authority area as either owner or tenant during the whole of the last 12 months.**

These rules do not apply to MSPs, MPs or MEPs. If you reside in Scotland but are a citizen of another EU state you can stand for election as an MSP, although you cannot seek election as an MP. Usually most candidates represent political parties, which have their own selection procedures to choose candidates for election.

You must register to vote if you are entitled to do so, although you don't have to vote in an election if you do not wish to.

Before an election all registered voters are sent a polling card, indicating the location and opening hours of their polling station.

If you cannot or do not wish to vote in person, you can arrange to have a postal vote. There are also special arrangements to help people who might have difficulty in casting their vote.

Usually elections are fought on a number of important issues, such as jobs, taxes or education; but occasionally, a candidate might campaign on a single issue, such as saving a local hospital from closure. For details of the main Scottish political parties, see **contacts**.

Political parties

Candidates standing for local, Scottish, UK and European elections generally represent a political party, although some candidates stand as an independent.

Local elections

There are 32 local councils in Scotland, each with the job of providing services including education, social care, waste management, and planning.

Councils are divided into a number of smaller units, known as wards; each ward has one or more councillors elected to represent that community. Council elections are held every four years using a form of proportional representation known as the single transferable vote, in which voters rank candidates in order of preference.

The next Scottish local elections will take place in 2016.

MSPs are elected to the Scottish Parliament every four years. The voting system for these elections is a form of proportional representation. Scotland is split into both constituencies and regions (a region is a group of constituencies).

Voters are given two ballot papers. On the first, they indicate who they would like to be the MSP for their constituency, and the person selected is the one who gets most votes. On the second, (the regional ballot paper) they vote for a political party (or an independent candidate), and these votes determine who will be the 'additional members' to represent voters in the region.

The system is designed to ensure that the number of MSPs a party has in Parliament reflects the proportion of people who voted for that party. There are currently 73 constituency MSPs and 56 regional list MSPs in the Scottish Parliament.

This system of voting has allowed the election of representatives from smaller parties, such as the Scottish Green Party. The last Scottish Parliament general election was held on Thursday, 5 May 2011. The election delivered the first majority government since the opening of Holyrood, with the Scottish National Party winning 69 seats. The next Scottish Parliament general election is due to be held on 5 May 2016.

MSPs MSPs debate and pass legislation on certain Scottish issues and work on Parliamentary Committees. They can ask questions on your behalf in the Scottish Parliament, or contact the appropriate Minister in the Scottish Government about an issue that you have raised.

having your say

General elections

The election of MPs to the UK Parliament is called a general election. Under the *Fixed-Term Parliaments Act 2011* a general election must take place every five years. The next general election is due to be held on the 7th May 2015.

However, a general election may still take place before this date if no party or coalition of parties can retain the confidence of the House of Commons, or if (under the new legislation) two thirds of MPs back a vote for an election.

Presently, there are 650 MPs sitting in Westminster, of which 59 represent Scottish constituencies.

Like MSPs, MPs debate and vote on legislation, work on committees, and can raise issues for you in the UK Parliament.

European elections

All countries that are members of the European Union elect MEPs to represent their interests in the European Parliament. Elections are held every five years using a system of proportional representation. Six MEPs represent Scottish constituencies.

Campaigning

If you feel strongly about something and want to get involved yourself, a library, Citizens Advice Bureau, or one of the organisations or websites listed in the contacts section can probably give you some of the information you need to make a start.

Campaigning can range from individual action to something more co-ordinated, as a member of a group. Writing a letter or email is the usual starting point – do your research, send it to a named person (the most senior within the organisation), keep a copy, and try to get others involved as well. If you can get a letter published in a newspaper, many more will know about your views, but do give your name and address – although you can ask the paper not to publish it.

having your say

Writing to your councillor, MSP, MP or MEP

If your problem is local, contact your local councillor through the council office. MSPs, MPs, or MEPs can best take up problems for which the Government in Edinburgh or London or the European Parliament are responsible. Most MSPs, MPs and some MEPs have local 'surgeries' for which no appointment is necessary. They are often held on a Friday or Saturday, and advertised in the local paper. You can also write to your MSP and MEP locally and your MP at the House of Commons. Many MSPs, MPs, and MEPs have their own websites.

You can find out the name of your local councillor, MSP, MP or MEP for your area at www.writetothem.com, and use the site to forward your message

Protest

If you wish to hold a protest march, you must abide by certain rules. You will generally need to give seven days' notice to the police and to the local authority of the area in which the march is to be held. The local authority can disallow the march altogether or stipulate, for example, the route or time at which it must take place.

Police officers in attendance at marches or public meetings can also give directions in order to prevent public disorder, damage to property, or intimidation.

Causing injury to other people or damage to their property remain offences, even if they are carried out as part of a protest.

Trespass

The *Criminal Justice and Public Order Act 1994* introduced the offence of aggravated trespass in response to the activities of hunt saboteurs. Although the Scottish Parliament passed legislation banning many types of hunting with dogs, it remains an offence to trespass on land where a lawful activity is taking place with the intention of intimidating, obstructing, or disrupting that activity.

Complaining

If you have a complaint about something you have bought or a service you have received, it's important to act quickly. Some companies, and many public services, have special procedures for dealing with complaints. If it's a public service, such as a hospital or benefits agency, you can ask to see a copy of their charter which shows the level of service you are entitled to expect. If your complaint is not dealt with properly, think about contacting your local councillor, MSP, or MP, particularly if your problem is over a public service. Try to:

- **act as quickly as possible;**
- **think carefully about what you want to achieve and, if necessary, get advice;**
- **make sure you talk or write directly to a person, such as the manager or director of services who has the authority to deal with your complaint;**
- **always find out the name of the person you are talking to;**
- **keep a record of phone calls or letters that you send;**
- **stick to the facts, and work out how the law can help you;**
- **state clearly what you want to be done, set a reasonable time within which this should happen, and get back in touch if they haven't met the deadline.**

If you are still unhappy with the way your problem has been handled, you may be able to take your case to an Ombudsman, see **contacts**, page 146.

Freedom of information

Under the *Freedom of Information (Scotland) Act 2002* and the *Environmental Information (Scotland) Regulations 2004*, you have the right to request any recorded information held by Scotland's public authorities and organisations that provide services for them.

Requests to the organisation

concerned (eg a school or hospital) must be made in writing - by letter, email or fax - or on audio or video tape. You must include your name and either your postal or email address, but you don't have to explain why you want the information or how you intend to use it.

Sometimes a request for information may be refused; however information can only be withheld in situations that have been specifically set out in the Act. If you are refused access, the authority must explain the reason for their decision.

You will receive a response to your request within 20 working days; most information is provided free of charge or for a small fee. If the information costs more that £100.00 to supply, a scale of charges is imposed, but you will be kept informed at all stages of the likely cost.

You also have a right of access to information held by UK public authorities under separate legislation – the *Freedom of Information Act 2000*. There is a similar process for access, see **contacts**.

Data protection

People collect personal information about you all the time. Your school, your GP, the local council, shops, your mobile phone company, your bank, your employer, the police and many others all keep records on you. Sometimes it's facts like your date of birth or how much you've spent on your mobile phone; sometimes it's opinions about whether you might pass or fail an exam.

All this is permitted under the *Data Protection Act 1998* as long as the people keeping and using the information follow various rules and procedures. The law tries to balance your right to privacy and fair treatment with other people's legitimate rights to keep and use information about you.

Very strict rules apply to other people collecting and using personal information such as your racial or ethnic origins, your political, religious, or other views, your sex life, any criminal offences and the state of your health. Usually your clear consent is needed before this information is stored or used.

One of the main protections you have is to be able to check what information is held about you and to get it put right if it's wrong. You are known as a 'data subject' and the law says you can apply to anyone to ask if they hold information about you and, if they do, what it is.

Applying for information

This is known as a 'subject access request' and you can write this in your own words, asking for all personal information held about you. Some organisations, like the police, have their own forms which you should use. You should identify yourself clearly and be as specific as possible about what you want to know. You can be asked to pay a fee. This is normally £10.00, but it can be as little as £2.00 (for credit information), or as much as £50.00 (for old handwritten medical records and some education records).

You should get a reply within 40 days (or 15 school days if the request is to a school) – and in some cases shorter times must be met. If you think the information is wrong you can require that it is changed and, if necessary, go to court for an order to correct it. Full details of your rights to check information held about you are available from the Information Commissioner's website, see **contacts**.

Judicial review

If a public body – like a government department, local authority, or hospital – makes a decision that seems to be fundamentally unfair, you can apply to have that decision reviewed in the Court of Session in Edinburgh. Known as judicial review, it's a way of having illegal or unreasonable decisions changed. The decisions of local councils, tribunals (eg immigration), and certain other bodies, such as the Scottish Football Association, can all be subjected to judicial review. A judicial review may be started only when all other avenues of complaint have been exhausted. It's a complicated and expensive process so, before doing anything, it's important to get advice from a solicitor who understands this area of law.

theeuropean
union

INDIVIDUALS
ENGAGING IN
SOCIETY

CitizenshipFoundation

membership

Twenty-eight countries are currently members of the European Union (EU).

Austria, Belgium, Bulgaria, Croatia, Cyprus, the Czech Republic, Denmark, Estonia, Finland, France, Germany, Greece, Hungary, Ireland, Italy, Latvia, Lithuania, Luxembourg, Malta, the Netherlands, Poland, Portugal, Romania, Slovakia, Slovenia, Spain, Sweden and the United Kingdom.

Membership negotiations have also taken place with Iceland, Macedonia, and Turkey – but it is expected that further enlargement will be slower than in recent years.

Origins   After the end of the Second World War, governments throughout Europe were determined not to repeat the horrors of the War, in which 50 million people had died.

Beginnings   In 1951, France, Belgium, Italy, Luxembourg, the Netherlands, and West Germany signed an agreement setting up the European Coal and Steel Community through which the coal and steel production of all six countries came under the control of a single European authority.

Those behind this plan believed that placing coal and steel production outside the control of individual states would greatly limit countries' ability to make weapons, and reduce the likelihood of another war. The UK was invited to join the ECSC, but declined.

Growth   In the early years co-operation was mainly designed to make it easier for member states to trade with one another. Gradually, the scope of the union has widened, and today covers many areas, including employment, the environment, transport, travel, foreign policy – and for 17 of the member states a common currency: the euro.

  use the law with care try talking first

The idea of European states forming a single market has always been central to the development of the European Union.

A single market means that goods, services, people, and money must be able to move freely between member states.

Over the last 30 years, member states have agreed all kinds of measures to make this possible, for example:

- **harmonising taxes and duties on products between member states;**
- **standardising technical and safety specifications of goods, so that goods made in one state meet the standards required in another;**
- **allowing EU citizens to travel, live, study, and work more-or-less wherever they wish within the EU.**

A single currency

The EU has also eased the movement of goods and people through the creation of a single currency, also sometimes called economic and monetary union (EMU).

The idea was first proposed in 1969, but the first significant steps were not taken until around 1990 when member states interested in moving towards a single currency began to prepare their economies for this process.

They were required to meet a number of conditions – usually described as convergence criteria – such as having low interest rates, keeping currency rates and prices stable, and keeping government expenditure within certain limits.

The euro

On 1 January 2002, after a transition period of two years, twelve of the then 15 EU member states moved to a single currency – the euro (€).

Today 17 of the 28 member states have euro banknotes and coins as their only legal tender. These are Austria, Belgium, Cyprus, Estonia, Finland, France, Germany, Greece, Ireland, Italy, Luxembourg, Malta, the Netherlands, Portugal, Slovakia, Slovenia, and Spain.

The euro is also used in some countries that are not EU members: Andorra, Kosovo, Montenegro, Monaco, San Marino, the Vatican City, and certain overseas French territories.

Britain and the euro

Britain, Denmark, and Sweden decided not to proceed with the single currency. Denmark voted against the euro in a referendum held in 2000, as did the people of Sweden in 2003. The British government has no declared plans to adopt the euro in the foreseeable future.

travel & work

Measures have been gradually introduced to help people move around the EU as easily as possible.

Travel
Citizens of an EU member state have the right to travel to any EU country, if they have a valid passport or identity card. This right may be restricted only for reasons of public order, public security, or public health.

EU citizens also have the right to travel within the EU with members of their family, but if they do not have EU nationality they may be required to have a visa, in addition to their passport.

Border controls
There are no customs checks for people travelling from one EU member state to another – although police controls on some frontiers remain, to check for terrorist activity, drug trafficking and organised crime.

In addition, identity checks for EU citizens have been abolished at many borders under what is called the Schengen Agreement. This allows people to travel from one country to another without having their passport or identity documents examined. Twenty-six member states, not including Britain and Ireland, have joined the group.

Health care
Citizens of EU member states who fall ill within another EU country are entitled to emergency treatment under that country's health care scheme.

The treatment is either free, or its cost is reduced for someone from Britain who can show the medical authorities their European Health Insurance Card (see **travel**, page 100).

A person who does not have an EHIC is still entitled to treatment, but may be asked to pay its full cost.

Help
An EU citizen who gets into difficulties in a country outside the EU may seek protection from the embassy or consulate of any EU member state.

For example, a British student arrested in a Russian city without a British consular office is entitled to help from the Swedish or Finnish consulate. For emergency services in any EU state, dial 112.

use the law with care try talking first

Work

British citizens are entitled to work in any EU country, and should be offered employment under the same conditions as citizens of that state. It would be against the law, for example, for an Italian firm to require British job applicants to have higher qualifications than their Italian counterparts – and vice versa.

Most jobs are open to all EU citizens. However, member states are allowed to insist that only nationals of that state hold certain public service posts, such as those in the police or armed forces. Anyone who wants to stay in another member state for more than three months may have to register with the local town hall or the police station.

Conditions

Generally speaking, a British citizen working in another EU member state has exactly the same employment rights and duties as everyone else in that country, and it is against the law for that person to be discriminated against on grounds of their nationality.

A British worker in Berlin, for example, should receive the same pay, employment opportunities, and health and safety protection as his or her German counterparts.

Qualifications

EU citizens who are qualified to work in a particular profession in their own country are also able to carry out that work in any other member state. However not all qualifications are automatically recognised – and applicants might need to check if their particular diploma or certificate is recognised.

Benefits

Citizens of EU member states are entitled to the same welfare and social security benefits as nationals of the country in which they are working. This covers sickness and maternity benefits, benefits for accidents at work, and unemployment. They also have the same rights, (where it is available), to accommodation, such as local authority housing.

Taxes

A person who lives and works in an EU member state must normally pay taxes in the same way as any other resident of that country. Levels of taxation vary from one EU state to another, but work is under way to try to find ways of harmonising taxation across member states.

goods

Customs duties

Generally speaking, goods purchased by people for their own use may be bought in other member states and brought back to Britain without having to pay extra tax or duties. People can bring in as much tobacco and alcohol from other EU member states as they like, as long as it is for personal use only and not for resale. However, some countries may impose limits from January 2014. Customs officials in the UK have the right to stop people and check this, and to confiscate any items they believe are not for personal use.

governing europe

The structure of the government of the European Union is not easy to understand – possibly because there are several organisations that help to determine EU policy.

THE EUROPEAN COUNCIL

The European Council is the name given to the regular meetings between the heads of the member states. They decide the issues the European Union should be concerned with. In the past this has included unemployment, drug trafficking, and enlarging the EU.

The Council of the European Union

This is one of the most influential bodies in the EU; along with the European Parliament, it has responsibility for making EU law. It consists of government ministers from each member state with powers to take decisions on how the EU is run, coordinate the broad economic policies of EU member countries, develop EU foreign policy, and negotiate with non-member states on behalf of the EU.

Decisions Until the mid 1980s, decisions by the Council of Ministers tended to have to be unanimous. If a nation disagreed, the measure could not be passed. Today the Council generally uses a system called qualified majority voting. Each member state has a certain number of votes, broadly reflecting the size of the country in terms of its population. For example, France, Germany, Italy, and the United Kingdom have 29 votes. Smaller countries, like Cyprus and Latvia, have four. However, this voting system may change in 2014.

The European Commission

Based in Brussels, the European Commission is rather like the civil service of the European Union, taking care of the day-to-day running of the organisation. Almost 25,000 people work for the Commission, making it one of Europe's largest institutions.

The Commission does several jobs; namely it:

- **drafts proposals for new EU laws or policies;**
- **checks that EU laws and treaties are properly applied;**
- **begins legal action against member states or businesses that it believes are not following EU law and;**
- **represents the EU on the international stage.**

EU Commissioners Each member state appoints one commissioner to take responsibility for running one particular aspect of EU business.

There are 27 commissioners in all. The current President, José Manuel Barroso, is from Portugal, and former leader of the House of Lords and Lord President of the Council, Catherine Ashton, is the UK representative. Currently she is the EU High Representative for Foreign Affairs and Security Policy. The commissioners are at the centre of EU government, rather like the Cabinet is in Britain.

use the law with care **try talking first**

THE EUROPEAN UNION

Changes to the EU

A draft EU Constitution was agreed by EU leaders in 2004 as a way of modernising the EU. It had to be approved by every EU country through either Parliament or a referendum, but in 2005 was rejected by France and the Netherlands. The idea of adopting the EU Constitution has now been dropped and in 2007 a new Reform Treaty was proposed instead. This, known as the Lisbon Treaty, was signed in December 2007, and carried out a number of reforms previously proposed in the EU Constitution. It came into force in December 2009.

The European Parliament

The European Parliament currently consists of 754 MEPs (Members of the European Parliament). The Parliament meets in Brussels, Luxembourg and Strasbourg. In the course of a month, MEPs usually meet for one week in Strasbourg, and for two weeks, on committee work, in Brussels. Parliamentary support staff are based in Brussels and Luxembourg.

Powers

Today, MEPs:
- **decide, together with the Council of Ministers, on EU law;**
- **control more than half the money that the EU spends;**
- **watch over the European Commission and approve the appointment of all Commissioners.**

Elections

The UK is allocated 73 of the 754 seats in the European Parliament. At the last elections in 2009, the Conservatives were the largest UK party in the European Parliament.

Voting

In the UK, as in all other EU member states, voting in the European Parliamentary elections is open to any EU citizen, provided they are on the local register of electors. Elections take place every five years.

Petitions

All EU citizens have the right to submit a petition to the President of the European Parliament, Martin Schulz MEP (the address is Rue Wiertz, B-1047, Brussels) or online, giving their view on a matter that is within the remit of the EU. The petition can be in any form, as long as it contains the sender's name, address, nationality, and signature.

BRIEF CASE: Fraud

In 1999, the European Parliament ordered an investigation into fraud and corruption by members of the European Commission. The report of the investigation was very critical of the Commission, and led to all 20 Commissioners resigning.

BRIEF CASE: Equal terms

Following a successful petition to the EU, the Greek authorities are now required to admit EU citizens to their museums under the same terms and conditions as Greek nationals.

law makers

Although the law in Scotland is still created and developed by MPs, MSPs and judges, our membership of the European Union requires all our laws to follow the treaties and agreements that we have made as members of the EU.

In this sense, European Union law has become the most important source of law in Britain. This is not to say that all our law comes from Europe, but it does mean that all our current and future laws must not break the principles set out in the treaties that we have signed.

■ BRIEF CASE: Mr Litster

Mr Litster worked for a Scottish company that became insolvent. At 3.30pm, one afternoon, Mr Litster and his colleagues were sacked. At 4.30pm that afternoon, a new company took over the business, and offered to take on all the old employees, but at a lower rate of pay.

The UK Government had adopted European Union laws to protect employees in these types of situations, but courts in the UK had previously said that these only applied if the employee was sacked at exactly the same time as the transfer of the business.

The House of Lords looked at the judgment of the European Court and decided that this was not correct, and that Mr Litster and his colleagues were entitled to compensation.

The European Union

Law created through our membership of the European Union normally reaches us in four ways – through treaties, regulations, directives, and court judgements.

Treaties

Treaties are agreements made between our government and other EU member states, which become incorporated into our law by Parliament. Treaties often contain broad agreements on which further action will be based. Sometimes, however, they include sections that can have a very specific effect on people's lives.

■ BRIEF CASE: Equal pay

The Treaty of Rome, signed in 1957, is the agreement on which the European Economic Community was established. Article 119 of the Treaty states that men and women should receive equal pay for equal work.

Regulations Regulations are the laws that put treaties into practice. Regulations automatically have effect in the UK, and no new national law is required.

Directives Directives, like regulations, are a means of putting an EU objective into practice, but member states are able to choose for themselves how this will be done.

■ BRIEF CASE: Equal access

An important section of the Treaty of Rome says that people should be able to move freely for work between member states. The regulations that have followed the Treaty require member states to introduce new laws to ensure this works. As a result, all member states needed to have laws granting visiting EU workers the same rights to education and housing as the citizens of their own state.

■ BRIEF CASE: In the know

In 2001, the EU issued a directive requiring companies operating in the EU to inform employees about any decision affecting their jobs – especially if it might lead to redundancy. This directive was made following a number of unexpected redundancies in France, made by several multinational companies. The UK was given seven years in which to implement the directive.

Court judgements The European Court of Justice considers all matters of European Union law. Located in Luxembourg, it is the most senior court in Europe and overrules all national courts. Member states must follow its decisions.

■ BRIEF CASE: John

Until relatively recently, UK winter fuel payments were paid to women from the age of 60, but not to men until they reached 65. This was challenged in the UK courts by retired postman John Taylor, who claimed it was unlawful discrimination.

The British High Court asked the European Court of Justice to deliver a judgement on this in the light of European Union law. The European Court announced that this practice did not follow EU law and that winter fuel payments should be given to men and women under the same terms

Getting information & advice

- Before you write, phone or ask for information, think carefully about exactly what you need to know.

- Don't be overlong in your explanation, keep to the most important details.

- If you are telephoning, you will probably first speak to a receptionist who may not be able to answer your question. Explain that you'd like to talk to someone about… (name the subject), and you should be put through. If they can't help, they may be able to give you the name of someone who can.

- It sometimes helps to put a few key words down on paper to remind you of what you want to say. You may also need a pen and paper to make a note of what you are told.

- It's a good idea to ask who you are talking to so, if you write or phone again, you know the name of the person you first spoke to.

The following names and details are arranged according to the chapters in the main part of the book and are just a few of the many organisations that can help with a whole range of law-related problems.

General

ChildLine Scotland, Templeton House, 62 Templeton Street, Glasgow G40 1DA, offers a free 24hr helpline, tel 0800 1111, for any child or young person in danger or distress, **www.childline.org.uk**.
If you are an adult and are worried about a child, you can contact the NSPCC helpline, tel 0808 800 5000, or visit their website, **www.nspcc.org.uk**.

Citizens Advice Bureau, usually known as the CAB, gives free, confidential and independent information and advice on all kinds of problems. You can enquire by phone or at one of their offices in most towns and cities. For your nearest CAB, see the local phone book, **www.adviceguide.org.uk/scotland**.

Gov.uk is the official website for UK government services and information, **www.gov.uk**.

Law Society of Scotland, 26 Drumsheugh Gardens, Edinburgh EH3 7HR, tel 0131 226 7411 email: lawscot@lawscot.org.uk, provides information on using a solicitor. The Society is also responsible for dealing with complaints made against solicitors, **www.lawscot.org.uk**.

Liberty, 21 Tabard Street, London SE1 4LA, is a campaigning organisation working to protect civil liberties and promote human rights. An advice line is open on Mon & Thurs, 6.30pm-8.30pm, Wed 12.30pm-2.30pm, tel 0845 123 2307, or 020 3145 0461, **www.liberty-humanrights.org.uk**. Liberty's other website, **www.yourrights.org.uk**, provides further information on human rights and the law.

The Ombudsman: if you have a problem with your local authority, a government department, the health service, an insurance company, a bank or building society or a legal service, and are not happy with how your complaint has been dealt with, you can refer your case to the relevant Ombudsman. You must first, however, have done everything you can to sort things out yourself with the person or organisation concerned. Your local CAB can explain how to submit a complaint, or you can find the ombudsman you require from the British and Irish Ombudsman Association, **www.bioa.org.uk**. If the Ombudsman decides your complaint is reasonable, the organisation responsible will be asked to do something about it. This means that you could get an apology or compensation, or that new procedures are put into place, so that the same thing doesn't happen again.

Scottish Child Law Centre, 54 East Crosscauseway, Edinburgh EH8 9HD, offers advice on a wide range of issues related to children and the law. An advice line operates Mon-Fri 9.30am-4.00pm, tel 0131 667 6333; freecall under 21s (landline) 0800 328 8970, (mob) 0300 330 14 21, **www.sclc.org.uk**.

Scottish Council of Law Reporting site provides extensive legal links to organisation able to provide further information on virtually every aspect of everyday law, **www.scottishlawreports.org.uk**.

The Scottish Government website provides information on the responsibilities of the devolved government of Scotland, **www.scotland.gov.uk**.

Scottish Legal Aid Board, 44 Drumsheugh Gardens, Edinburgh EH3 7SW, tel 0131 226 7061; legal aid allows people to get help with their legal problems; legal aid information line, tel 0845 122 86 86, **www.slab.org.uk**.

use the law with care try talking first

Scottish Public Services Ombudsman, 4 Melville Street, Edinburgh EH3 7NS, tel 0800 377 7330, deals with complaints about public services in Scotland including councils, the National Health Service, housing associations, most water and sewage providers, prisons, the Scottish Government and its agencies and departments, universities and colleges and most Scottish public authorities, **www.spso.co.uk**.

Solicitors give advice on legal problems, take action for you on your behalf and represent you in many courts or tribunals. There are solicitors' offices in every town and city in Scotland. Many solicitors take publicly funded or conditional fee cases, and some will give you a free introductory interview. However when you first make contact, it's important to check that legal aid is available and, if not, ask how much the work will cost. Choosing the right firm of solicitors is important. The Law Society of Scotland or your local CAB can give you the name of firms specialising in cases involving your particular problem. A solicitor may engage an advocate to appear in a higher court; for more information on this, see **www.advocates.org.uk**.

Young Scot provides a wide range of services to people aged 11-26 years, in collaboration with the Scottish Government and all local councils. The Young Scot National Entitlement Card provides discounts on a wide range of activities, including travel and transport, food, clothes, cinema etc, **www.youngscot.org**.

Life

HEALTH

Mental Welfare Commission for Scotland, Thistle House, 91 Haymarket Terrace, Edinburgh, EH12 5HE, tel 0131 313 8777, can provide information and advice on mental health law for patients and carers. A helpline is open Mon-Thurs 9am-5pm and Fri 9:30am-4.30pm., tel free 0800 389 6809, **www.mwcscot.org.uk**.

NHS 24, the 24-hour health information and self-care advice service for Scotland, tel 08454 24 24 24, **www.nhs24.com**.

Samaritans, will talk to anyone feeling desperate, lonely or suicidal. You can say what you like, you need not give your name, it's entirely confidential. They can be reached by phone at any time, every day of the year. The contact number is 08457 90 90 90, lines are open 24 hours a day, seven days a week, **www.samaritans.org.uk**.

Scottish Association for Mental Health, Brunswick House, 51 Wilson Street, Glasgow G1 1UZ, tel 0141 530 1000, provides information and support on mental health. A freephone information service is open Mon-Fri, 2-4pm, tel 0800 917 3466, **www.samh.org.uk**.

DRUGS AND ADDICTION

Drinkline Scotland is a helpline for those concerned about their drinking or that of their friends or family, open Mon-Fri 9am-8pm, Sat & Sun 11am-4pm, tel 0800 7314 314.

Drinksmarter is a Scottish website with information and resources to help people manage their drinking habits, **www.drinksmarter.org**.

Know The Score, information and advice on drugs and the law from Drug Advice Scotland, a helpline is open seven days a week, 8am-11pm, tel 0800 587 5879, **http://knowthescore.info**.

Release, Ferguson House, 5th Floor, 124 -128 City Road, London EC1V 2NJ provides information and advice on drugs and the law, it also offers a telephone help and advice open Mon-Fri 11am-1pm and 2-4pm, tel 020 7324 2989, **www.release.org.uk**.

SEX, CONTRACEPTION, PREGNANCY

British Association for Adoption and Fostering (BAAF) 113 Rose Street, Edinburgh EH2 3DT, tel 0131 226 9270, provides advice and information for those thinking of having their baby adopted, **www.baaf.org.uk/scotland**.

British Pregnancy and Advisory Service, has over 40 centres nationwide able to provide pregnancy tests, consultation and emergency contraception, and to undertake abortions, tel 08457304030 or (mobiles and outside the UK) +441789508211, **www.bpas.org**.

Brook Advisory Centres, offer free and confidential advice and counselling on sex and contraception for young people under 25, covering the whole of the UK – although their only centre in Scotland is in Inverness. A nationwide advice line for young people under 25 is open Mon- Fri 9am-6pm, tel 0808 802 1234, **www.brook.org.uk**.

Caledonia Youth, 5 Castle Terrace, Edinburgh EH1 2DP, tel 0131 229 3596, provides free confidential advice and counselling on personal relationships and sexual wellbeing for young people under 25, **www.caledoniayouth.org**.

fpa provides information on contraception and sexual health and has clinics throughout the UK; there is a confidential helpline, Mon-Fri 9am-3pm, tel 0845 122 8690, **www.fpa.org.uk**.

Life UK, LIFE House, 1 Mill Street, Leamington Spa, Warwickshire CV31 1ES, is a pro-life charity offering support to anyone facing a crisis pregnancy, who has lost a child during pregnancy, or who has had an abortion; helpline tel, 0808 802 5433, **www.lifecharity.org.uk**.

Stonewall Scotland, Mansfield Traquair Centre, 15 Mansfield Place, Edinburgh EH3 6BB, tel, 131 474 8019, offers information and advice for gay men, lesbians and bisexuals, **www.stonewallscotland.org.uk**.

HIV AND AIDS

Avert, 4 Brighton Road, Horsham, West Sussex, RH13 5BA, an international HIV & AIDS charity base in the UK, providing a wide range of information on HIV & AIDS, **www.avert.org**.

HIV Scotland, 18 York Place, Edinburgh, EH1 3EP, tel 0131 558 3713, provides information and advice on HIV, **www.hivscotland.com**.

Positively UK, a national charity championing the rights of people living with HIV, providing information and advice, **www.positivelyuk.org**.

Terrence Higgins Trust Scotland, 134 Douglas Street, Glasgow G2 4HF, tel 0141 332 3838, a national charity providing support and information for people with and affected by HIV and AIDS, **www.tht.org.uk**.

Safety

ChildLine Scotland, Templeton House, 62 Templeton Street, Glasgow G40 1DA, offers a free 24hr helpline, tel 0800 1111, for any child or young person in danger or distress, **www.childline.org.uk**.
If you are an adult and are worried about a child, you can contact the NSPCC helpline, tel 0808 800 5000, or visit their website, **www.nspcc.org.uk**.

Criminal Injuries Compensation Authority, Tay House, 300 Bath Street, Glasgow G2 4LN, administers the Criminal Injuries Compensation Scheme which operates in Scotland, England and Wales, and is a government-funded scheme to compensate victims of violent crime. Information and application forms available by post, or call the CICA, tel 0300 003 3601, Mon-Fri 8.30am-5pm, except Wed, open 10am-5pm, **www.cica.gov.uk**.

Equality and Human Rights Commission works to make people aware of their human rights and to eliminate unfair discrimination. Information and guidance are available from its publications and the EHRC website, **www.equalityhumanrights.com/scotland**.

Kidscape offers information and advice to children and parents on ways of dealing with and preventing bullying and other forms of abuse, an anti-bullying helpline for parents of bullied children is open Mon-Thurs, 10am-4pm, tel 08451 205 204, **www.kidscape.org.uk**.

National Stalking Helpline provides guidance and information to anybody who is currently or has previously been affected by harassment or stalking. A helpline operates Mon-Fri 9.30am-4pm, except Wed 1-4pm, tel 0808 802 0300, **www.stalkinghelpline.org**.

Rape Crisis Scotland, 46 Bath Street, Glasgow G2 1HG, tel 0141 331 4180, 41 248 8848 provides information and support for anyone affected by sexual violence. A free helpline operates everyday 6pm-midnight, tel 08088 01 03 02, **www.rapecrisisscotland.org.uk**.

Scottish Court Service, Saughton House, Broomhouse Drive, Edinburgh EH11 3XD, tel 0131 444 3300, provides information for those attending or visiting a court along with details of how certain court processes work and guidance on taking action through the courts, **www.scotcourts.gov.uk**.

Survivor Scotland provides information and guidance for people who have suffered childhood abuse, **www.survivorscotland.org**.

Suzy Lamplugh Trust, National Centre for Personal Safety, 218 Strand, London WC2R 1AT, tel 020 7091 0014, a campaigning organisation providing information and guidance on personal safety, **www.suzylamplugh.org**.

Victim Support Scotland, 15-23 Hardwell Close, Edinburgh EH8 9RX, tel 0131 668 4486, provides emotional support, practical help and essential information to victims, witnesses and others affected by crime. A helpline operates Mon-Fri 8am-8pm, tel 0845 603 9213, **www.victimsupportsco.org.uk**.

use the law with care **try talking first**

Education

Education Law Unit, Govan Law Centre, 47 Burleigh Street, Glasgow G51 3LB, can respond to queries about all aspects of education law in Scotland, tel 0141 445 1955, **www.edlaw.org.uk**.

Education Scotland, the official Government education website, **www.educationscotland.gov.uk**. Details of policy and law can be obtained with key words via the search box, eg attendance, exclusion etc, or see **Parentzone** for more general details of school organisation.

Kidscape offers information and advice to children and parents on ways of dealing with and preventing bullying and other forms of abuse, an anti-bullying helpline for parents of bullied children is open Mon-Thurs, 10am-4pm, tel 08451 205 204, **www.kidscape.org.uk**.

My World of Work provides careers guidance and advice on CVs, job search and interviews, provided by Skills Development Scotland, **www.myworldofwork.co.uk**.

Schoolhouse Home Education Association, c/o Eighteen and Under, Room 10, 1 Victoria Road, Dundee DD1 2EL, tel 01307 463 120, provides information and advice for people choosing to educate their children out of school, **www.schoolhouse.org.uk**.

Scottish Catholic Education Service, 75 Craigpark, Glasgow, G31 2HD, provides information on Catholic schools throughout Scotland, **www.sces.uk.com**.

Scottish Council of Independent Schools, 61 Dublin Street, Edinburgh EH3 6NL, tel 0131 556 2316 for information on education in the independent sector, **www.scis.org.uk**.

Scottish Qualifications Authority is the national body for development, accreditation, assessment and certification of qualifications other than degrees, tel 0345 279 1000, **www.sqa.org.uk**.

Work and training

ACAS (the Advisory, Conciliation & Arbitration Service), provides a wide range of information on employment law and procedures on its website, **www.acas.org.uk**. It also runs a helpline for people seeking information on employment rights, rules, & issues, tel 08457 47 47 47, open Mon-Fri, 8am-8pm; Sat, 9am-1pm.

Equality Advisory and Support Service provides information advice and support on discrimination and human rights issues in England, Scotland and Wales, tel 0808 800 0082, Mon-Fri 9am-8pm, Sat 10am-2pm, **www.equalityadvisoryservice.com**.

Equality and Human Rights Commission works to make people aware of their human rights and to eliminate unfair discrimination. Information and guidance are available from its publications and the EHRC website, **www.equalityhumanrights.com/scotland**.

Health & Safety Executive (HSE) is responsible for checking and maintaining health and safety at work throughout the UK. Its website contains a wide range of law-related information, together with details of who to contact if you have a health and safety problem at work, **www.hse.gov.uk**.

My World of Work provides careers guidance and advice on CVs, job search and interviews, provided by Skills Development Scotland, **www.myworldofwork.co.uk**.

Pay & Work Rights Helpline provides information on the national and agricultural minimum wage, and for people working for an employment agency or gangmaster. The Helpline is open Mon-Fri, 8am-8pm; Sat, 9am-1pm, tel 0800 917 2368, **www.gov.uk/pay-and-work-rights-helpline**.

TUC (Trades Union Council) provides detailed information on rights and responsibilities at work, including those for young workers, **www.worksmart.org.uk**.

Money

Association of British Insurers, Consumer Information Dept., 51 Gresham Street, London EC2V 7HQ, tel 020 7600 3333, for leaflets and further information on insurance, **www.abi.org.uk**.

Benefits information is available from the official government website, **www.gov.uk**, link to benefits.

HM Revenue & Customs provide information on tax, national insurance, and some benefits on their website, **www.hmrc.gov.uk**, including guidance on obtaining a tax refund. See also the Government site, **www.gov.uk**.

Mailing Preference Service enables people to have their name removed from direct mail lists, **www.mpsonline.org.uk**.

Money Advice Service provides further guidance on benefits, saving, borrowing and insurance, **www.moneyadviceservice.org.uk**.

National Debtline Scotland offers confidential and independent advice on how to deal with debt problems, tel (free) 0808 8084000, Mon-Fri 9am-9pm, Sat 9.30am-1pm, **www.nationaldebtline.co.uk/scotland**.

PhonepayPlus, Clove Building, 4 Maguire Street, London SE1 2NQ, regulates products and services that are charged to users' phone bills or pre-pay accounts. Their role is to respond to questions and complaints about premium rate phone services like helplines, news alerts, interactive games etc. If you have a complaint, or are seeking information or advice about any of these services, call 0800 500 212, Mon-Fri, 9am-5pm, or go online at **www.phonepayplus.org.uk**.

Telephone Preference Service enables you to opt out of receiving unsolicited sales and marketing calls, **www.tpsonline.org.uk**.

Trading Standards offices are in almost every large town and city, and give free advice on a wide range of consumer problems. The address of your nearest office is available from the phone book, under 'T', your local council website, or from **www.tradingstandards.gov.uk**.

Turn2us provides detailed information on access to benefits and grants, **www.turn2us.org.uk**.

Family

Birth Link, Family Care, 21 Castle Street, Edinburgh EH2 3DN. Tel: (0131) 225 6441 a registered charity offering a range of services for people with a Scottish connection separated by adoption, **www.birthlink.org.uk**.

British Association for Adoption and Fostering (BAAF) 113 Rose Street, Edinburgh EH2 3DT, tel 0131 226 9270, provides advice and information for those thinking of adopting or fostering, **www.baaf.org.uk/scotland**.

ChildLine Scotland, Templeton House, 62 Templeton Street, Glasgow G40 1DA, offers a free 24hr helpline, tel 0800 1111, for any child or young person in danger or distress, **www.childline.org.uk**. If you are an adult and are worried about a child, you can contact the **NSPCC** helpline, tel 0808 800 5000, or visit their website, **www.nspcc.org.uk**.

Children 1st, 83 Whitehouse Loan, Edinburgh EH9 1AT, tel 0131 446 2300, runs a range of services promoting the safety of children and young people, with details of help and advice available for children, young people, parents and carers, **www.children1st.org.uk**.

Kidscape, 2 Grosvenor Gardens, London SW1W 0DH, tel 020 7730 3300, provides free information and advice to children, their parents/carers and those who work with them, on bullying, abuse and keeping safe. A helpline, tel 08451 205 204, is available Mon-Thurs, 10am-4pm, primarily for parents of children who are being bullied, **www.kidscape.org.uk**.

Missing People is a charity that helps to find missing people and provides support for their family and friends. It also provides a 24hr Runaway Helpline; calling or texting is free, even if you have no credit left on your mobile phone, call or text 116 000, **www.missingpeople.org.uk**.

National Records of Scotland, Change of Name Unit, New Register House, Edinburgh EH1 3YT, tel 0131 314 4404, gives details of process and application forms to record a change of name, **www.gro-scotland.gov.uk**.

One-Parent Families Scotland, 13 Gayfield Square, Edinburgh EH1 3NX, tel 0131 556 3899 gives help and advice on a wide range of issues, including disability, employment, education, family support, lone fathers and a free lone parent helpline, tel open Mon-Thurs 9.30am-4pm and Fri 9.30am-4.30pm, **www.opfs.org.uk**.

Scottish Child Law Centre, 54 East Crosscauseway, Edinburgh EH8 9HD, offers advice on a wide range of issues related to children and the law. An advice line operates Mon-Fri 9.30am-4pm, tel 0131 667 6333; freecall under 21s (landline) 0800 328 8970, (mob) 0300 330 14 21, **www.sclc.org.uk**.

Scottish Domestic Abuse Helpline for anyone affected by domestic or sexual abuse, open 24 hours, tel 0800 027 1234, **www.scottishdomesticabusehelpline.org.uk**.

Scottish Women's Aid, 2nd Floor, 132 Rose street, Edinburgh EH2 3JD, tel 0131 226 6606, provide help and advice for anyone experiencing domestic abuse, **www.scottishwomensaid.org.uk**.

use the law with care try talking first

Home

Crisis Skylight Edinburgh, Crichton House, 4 Crichton's Close, Edinburgh EH8 8DT, a national charity for single homeless people, tel 0131 337 5507 **http://www.crisis.org.uk**, follow the link to Edinburgh.

Edinburgh Housing Advice Partnership provides information and advice to tenants and home owners to help them avoid becoming homeless and to secure housing support, tel 0845 302 4607, Mon-Fri, 9am-5pm, **www.ehap.org.uk**.

The Foyer Federation 5-9 Hatton Wall, London EC1N 8HX tel 020 7430 2212, a UK-wide youth homeless charity providing accommodation, education and training opportunities for 16-25 year olds with housing needs. Contact Aberdeen Foyer, tel 01224 373 880, **www.aberdeenfoyer.com**.

Legal Services Agency has offices in Glasgow, Edinburgh and Greenock offering housing and other law-related advice, tel 0800 316 8450 or 0141 353 3354, **www.lsa.org.uk**.

Shelter Scotland, 4th floor, Scotiabank House, 6 South Charlotte Street, Edinburgh EH2 4AW, campaigns to improve the housing conditions and rights of private tenants. The website, **http://scotland.shelter.org.uk,** provides extensive hosing advice and there is an advice open Mon-Fri, 9am-5pm, tel 0808 800 4444. Shelter also has local centres in East Lothian, the Scottish Borders and North Lanarkshire.

Private Rented Housing Panel, Europa Building, 450 Argyle Street, Glasgow G2 8LH, tel 0141 242 0142, works to solve problems between landlords and tenants, with their website containing detailed guidance on both sides' rights and responsibilities, **www.prhpscotland.gov.uk**.

Leisure

CitizenCard, 36 Bromells Road, London SW4 0BG, can provide a photo-ID card and proof of age for a fee of £13.00 (2013). Application forms are available from supermarkets, post offices, off licences, newsagents or online, **www.citizencard.com**.

Outdoor Access Scotland, for information on rights of access outdoors, **www.outdooraccess-scotland.com**.

Scottish Environment Protection Agency (SEPA), has a 24hr emergency pollution hotline 0800 80 70 60. For general enquiries contact SEPA Corporate Office, Erskine Court, Castle Business Park, Stirling FK9 4TR, tel: 01786 457 700. **www.sepa.org.uk**.

Scottish Natural Heritage, Great Glen House, Leachkin Road, Inverness IV3 8NW, tel 01463 725 000, for information on access to land and inland water for outdoor recreation, **www.snh.gov.uk**.

Scottish Society for the Prevention of Cruelty to Animals Kingseat Road, Halbeath, Dunfermline KY11 8RY; to report an injured or distressed animal write to the above address or call 03000 999 999, open 7am-11pm, **www.scottishspca.org**.

Validate UK, Main House, Bishop's Yard, Corbridge, Northumberland NE45 5LA, tel 01434 634 996, operates a national, approved proof of age scheme, for a fee of £15.00. Application forms available by phone, post, or downloadable from **www.validateuk.co.uk**.

Young Scot Card, available free to anyone aged 11-26, with a PASS hologram indicating proof of age, **www.youngscot.org/card**.

Travel and transport

ABTA (The Association of British Travel Agents), 30 Park Street, London SE1 9EQ, for information and advice on problems with a package holiday, tel 020 3117 0599 , **www.abta.com**, email: information@abta.org.uk.

Civil Aviation Authority, Scottish Office, First Floor, Kings Park House, Laurelhill Business Park, Stirling FK7 9JQ, tel 01786 457 400, for information and advice on travel-related problems, **www.caa.co.uk**: home page - resolving travel problems.

Department for Transport, 33 Horseferry Road, London SW1 4DR, tel 0300 330 3000, for information on transport and motoring regulations, **www.dft.gov.uk**.

Driving Standards Agency, PO Box 280, Newcastle-Upon-Tyne NE99 1FP, Customer Service Centre, tel 0300 200 1122, for information on driving tests, compulsory basic training, and other motoring regulations, email: customer.services@dsa.gsi.gov.uk, **www.dsa.gov.uk**.

Driver and Vehicle Licensing Agency, DVLA, Licensing Centre, Longview Road, Swansea SA6 7JL for enquiries about driving licences, tax discs or the registration details of a particular vehicle go to; driver enquiries, tel 0300 790 6801; vehicle enquiries, tel 0300 790 6802; **www.dvla.gov.uk**.

European Youth Card, for discount on travel and transport, **www.eyca.org**.

International Youth Travel Card is available from student travel organisations.

National Express Ltd, Customer Relations, PO Box 9854, Birmingham B16 8XN, for information on coach travel and discount travel schemes, tel 0871 781 8178, **www.nationalexpress.com**.

Royal Society for the Prevention of Accidents (RoSPA), 43, Discovery Terrace, Heriot-Watt University Research Park, Edinburgh EH14 4AP, tel 0131 449 9379, information on safety on the road and in the home, **www.rospa.com**.

Young Scot Card, for special deals on transport, **www.youngscot.org/card**.

16-25 Railcard, National Railcards, PO Box 11638, Laurencekirk AB30 9AJ, for details of obtaining a Railcard, eligibility and benefits, **www.16-25railcard.co.uk**.

European Health Insurance Card (EHIC) for details about the card and to make an application, **www.scot.nhs.uk**; for enquiries contact the Overseas Healthcare Team, tel 0191 218 1999.

Police and courts

Citizens Advice Bureau (CAB), have trained staff who can give free legal advice and suggest solicitors able to deal with your particular problem. See **General** section, for contact details.

Judiciary of Scotland, provides extensive information about the work of the courts, the people involved, and guidance on attending court as a witness or observer, www.scotland-judiciary.org.uk.

Police Investigations and Review Commissioner, Hamilton Business Park, Caird Park, Hamilton ML3 0QA, tel (free) 0808 178 5577, an independent body responsible for the oversight of Police Scotland and the Scottish Police Authority. For information on how to make a complaint about the police, see http://www.scotland.police.uk/assets/pdf/1 38327/147514/complaints-about-the-police-guide?view=Standard

Police Scotland, www.scotland.police.uk, for information about the police service in Scotland, including numbers to ring in an emergency (999) and when the call is less urgent or to your local police station (101). If you wish to know more making a complaint against the police, follow the link on the home page.

Scottish Court Service, Saughton House, Broomhouse Drive, Edinburgh EH11 3XD, tel 0131 444 3300. The Scottish Court website provides full details of court, tribunal and justice services in Scotland, together with details of court locations, www.scotcourts.gov.uk.

Scottish Legal Aid Board, 44 Drumsheugh Gardens, Edinburgh EH3 7SW, tel 0131 226 7061. Legal aid allows people who would not otherwise be able to afford it to get help for their legal problems. There is a Legal Aid Helpline, tel 0845 122 8686, open 7 days a week 7am-11pm, www.slab.org.uk.

Victims of Crime in Scotland provides step-by-step information on the justice process, as it affects both young people and adults, with details of other sources of help and advice, www.victimsofcrimeinscotland.org.uk.

Law, government and human rights

POLITICAL PARTIES

Scottish Conservatives, Scottish Conservative Central Office, 67 Northumberland Street, Edinburgh EH3 6JG, tel 0131 524 0030, **www.scottishconservatives.com**.

Scottish Green Party, Bonnington Mill, 72 Newhaven Road, Edinburgh, EH6 5QG, tel 08700 772 207, **www.scottishgreens.gov.uk**.

Scottish Labour Party, 290 Bath Street , Glasgow G2 4RE tel 0141 572 6900, **www.scottishlabour.org.uk**.

Scottish Liberal Democrats, 4 Clifton Terrace, Edinburgh EH12 5DR, tel 0131 337 2314, **www.scotlibdems.org.uk**.

Scottish National Party, Gordon Lamb House, 3 Jackson's Entry, Edinburgh EH8 8PJ, tel 0800 633 5432, **www.snp.org**.

Scottish Socialist Party, Suite 370, 4th Floor, Central Chambers, 93 Hope St, Glasgow G2 6LD, tel 0141 221 7470, **www.scottishsocialistparty.org**.

Solidarity, PO Box 7565, Glasgow G42 2DN, **www.new.solidarityscotland.org**.

GENERAL

House of Commons Information Office, House of Commons, London SW1A 2TT, tel 020 7219 4272. A public information service on the working and proceedings of Parliament. **www.parliament.uk/mps-lords-and-offices/offices/commons/hcio/**.

Information Commissioner's Office, Wycliffe House, Water Lane, Wilmslow, Cheshire SK9 5AF tel 0303 123 1113, has responsibility for overseeing the workings of the Data Protection Act 1998 and the Freedom of Information Act 2000, **www.ico.gov.uk**.

Scottish Human Rights Commission, 4 Melville Street, Edinburgh EH3 7NS tel 0131 240 2989, **www.scottishhumanrights.com**. For information on the Human Rights Act, refer to the Ministry of Justice site, **www.justice.gov.uk/human-rights**.

Scottish Information Commissioner, Kinburn Castle, Doubledykes Road, St Andrews, Fife KY16 9DS, tel 01334 464610, has responsibility for overseeing the workings of the Freedom of Information (Scotland) Act 2002. **www.itspublicknowledge.info**.

Scottish Parliament, Edinburgh EH99 1SP, tel 0131 348 5000 / 0800 092 7500, **www.scottish.parliament.uk**.

Scottish Youth Parliament aims to be the collective national youth voice for all young people in Scotland, aged 14-25, **www.syp.org.uk**.

European Union

The Council of Europe, works to create respect for human rights, democracy and the rule of law throughout Europe. For further information, see **www.cec.org.uk**, or contact the Council of Europe, Avenue de L'Europe, 67075 Strasbourg Cedex, France, tel +33(0)3 88 41 20 33, email: infopoint@coe.int.

European Commission provides a portal for a very wide range of information about the European Union. For questions about the EU call Europe Direct from anywhere in Europe, tel 00 800 67 89 10 11, Mon-Fri, 9am-6.00pm, CET. For advice on life, work and travel in the EU see Your Europe, **http://ec.europa.eu/youreurope/citizens/index_en.htm**.

European Parliament Information Office in Edinburgh, The Tun, 4 Jackson's Entry, Holyrood Road Edinburgh EH8 8PJ, tel 0131 557 7866, epedinburgh@europarl.europa.eu, **www.europarl.org.uk**, provides information about the structures and activities of the European Parliament, European elections and your local MEPs.

European Youth Forum (EYF) represents youth organisations from all over Europe, channeling information and opinions between young people and decision makers, **www.youthforum.org**.

Organising Bureau of School Students Unions (OBESSU) coordinates cooperation between national organisations of school students in Europe, Rue de la Sablonnière 20, 1000 Brussels, Belgium, tel +32 (0) 264 72 390, **www.obessu.org**.